BUTTERFLIES

OF BRITAIN AND EUROPE

BUTTERFLIES
OF BRITAIN AND EUROPE

ALLAN WATSON

Illustrated by
Alan Male, David Wright
and Bernard Robinson

Consultant
David Carter

This edition published in 1992 by Rainbow Books,
Elsley House, 24–30 Great Titchfield Street, London W1P 7AD.

Originally published in 1981 by Kingfisher Books as a Kingfisher Guide to Butterflies.

ISBN 1 871745 89 6

Printed and bound in Italy.

CONTENTS

INTRODUCTION

Butterflies are insects, a group that outnumbers all the other animal species put together and has existed on earth several millions of years longer than human beings. There are probably between 15,000 and 20,000 different kinds of butterflies in the world, and about 300 to 400 species in Europe as a whole. In western Europe, from the Alps northwards (but also the island of Corsica), there are 255 species; all are mentioned in this book. Unless otherwise stated, the butterflies illustrated are adult males.

Structure and Colour

All butterflies are covered with thousands of tiny *scales*, overlapping each other like the tiles on a roof. These scales are easily detached and produce a buttery feel that perhaps gave rise to the name *butterfly*. Hidden underneath the scales is the *skeleton* of the butterfly. This is a fairly hard outer shell, rather like a suit of armour, and has joints to allow movement between the segments of the legs, antennae and body.

The adult butterfly has a head, two large eyes, a *proboscis* for sucking up liquid food, and two *antennae*, which the butterfly uses to recognize all kinds of scents. Behind the head there is a muscular *thorax*, to which the three pairs of legs and two pairs of wings are attached. The rear part of the body is the *abdomen*, which encloses most of the gut and reproductive organs and has at its tip the egg-laying apparatus in the female and the mating equipment in the male.

The most noticeable feature of butterflies is their distinctively patterned *wings*. These enable them to fly, help the two sexes of a species to recognize one another, and absorb heat from the sun like solar panels. The Monarch and other poisonous species have conspicuously coloured wings as a reminder to enemies to keep away, but the Peacock and many other

THE PARTS OF A BUTTERFLY

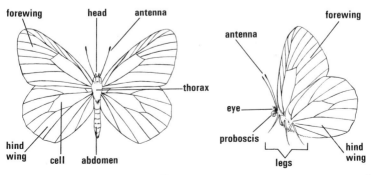

A Cabbage White feeding on a flower.

9

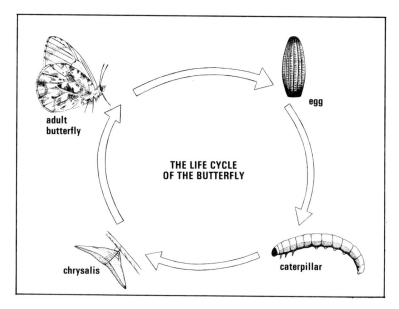

adult butterfly

egg

THE LIFE CYCLE OF THE BUTTERFLY

chrysalis

caterpillar

butterflies have the underside of the wings sombrely coloured so that they merge into their surroundings when the wings are closed. Large eye-spots, like those on the upper side of the Peacock, probably frighten small birds when the wings are opened and the bird suddenly sees what appear to be four large eyes staring at it.

Internally, like human beings, a butterfly has a brain, a gut through which food passes, a blood circulatory system, a reproductive system and, unlike humans, a fine network of air passages (*tracheae*) that lead from holes on the outside of the body (*spiracles*). This method of getting oxygen to the tissues is less efficient than in humans, so that butterflies and other insects are relatively small in size.

The *caterpillar* is similar in basic form to the adult, but lacks wings and scales, and has biting jaws instead of a proboscis, and several tiny eyes instead of two large ones. Many caterpillars are green and difficult to see amongst the leaves of their foodplants, but others practise a more complicated deception, like that of the White Admiral, which disguises itself with its own droppings.

The *chrysalis*, when fully formed, is much like a mummified adult and is enclosed in a generally rigid outer covering.

The Life-history of a Butterfly

There are four stages in a butterfly's life: egg, caterpillar, chrysalis and adult. Whether it moves or not, each stage involves intensive activity during the warm months of the year. Whilst some butterflies have several generations a year, many take twelve months to complete one full life-cycle, and some Arctic and alpine butterflies, for example the Large Ringlet, need two years to complete the cycle.

The Egg Stage is a growing stage, not so much in size, but in development from a single microscopic cell to a minute, but complete, caterpillar. Each female butterfly lays many eggs, which are usually firmly glued down on a leaf or bud of the foodplant, although the Marbled White and a few other grass-feeders scatter their eggs over the foodplant while in flight. Some species lay their eggs singly, others in clusters, whilst the Map Butterfly lays its eggs in hanging rows like beads on a string. The eggs of most butterflies hatch after a few days, the young caterpillar eating at least part of its shell on its way out. In other species, the eggs remain dormant until the spring of the following year, or the caterpillar develops inside the egg-shell but does not hatch out until after the winter.

The Caterpillar Stage There is usually some change in shape and colour during this stage but always an impressive increase in size and weight. The caterpillar's function is to feed, and some, like the Black Hairstreak, do so night and day. As it develops, it has to *moult*, or shed its skin, to allow for further growth. The new skin develops underneath the old one and is sometimes differently coloured. Some species feed on particular groups of plants; many Blues feed only on Pea-family plants (*Legumes*) and some Fritillaries only on Violets (*Viola*). Caterpillars emerging from eggs laid in batches usually spin a silken web and feed together (for example, the Small Tortoiseshell). Many Skippers shelter in a silken tube when not feeding. The Large Blue changes from a vegetarian to a carnivorous diet of ant grubs inside ants' nests. The caterpillars of many other Blues, Hairstreaks and Coppers are accompanied by ants that feed on a sugary liquid produced by a honeygland on the caterpillar's back, but they are not taken into the ants' nests. Many caterpillars overwinter and feed again in the spring before finding a place in which to change into a chrysalis.

The Chrysalis Stage The amazing transformation into a winged butterfly takes place during this stage, although there is no sign of this activity outside the hard outer casing of the chrysalis. Many chrysalids hang upside-down from a group of hooks at the tail end (Danaids, Nymphalids and many Browns), or are attached head upwards by tail hooks and a girdle of silk around the middle (Swallowtails, Whites, Metalmarks and most Lycaenids), whilst others are formed inside a cocoon of silk and leaves (Skippers) or silk and soil particles (some Browns). In some species the chrysalis overwinters (for example the autumn generation of the Large White), whilst in the Small Tortoiseshell and others the adult butterfly may emerge in less than two weeks.

The Adult Stage After breaking out of the chrysalis case and expanding its wings, the adult's purpose in life is to find a mate. Once mating has taken place and the eggs have been fertilized, the female must find the right foodplants on which to lay her eggs and complete the cycle. A few butterflies overwinter in the adult stage, for example the Peacock and the Brimstone.

Where to Find Butterflies

Butterflies occur in a variety of places in Europe, from dry heaths and sand-dunes to bogs and marshes, in open grassland and dense woodland, at sea-level and in the mountains to above 2,000 metres, and from the Mediterranean to the northernmost tip of Scandinavia. Many are confined to particular habitats, like the Cranberry Fritillary, which occurs only in bogs and similar wet places, and the Chalk-hill Blue, which is restricted to grassy slopes of chalk and limestone hills. Other specialists are the Speckled Wood, a butterfly of shady woodland glades; the Purple Emperor, a species of the tree-tops; and the Orange-tip, which prefers hedgerows and the edges of woodland. The Dewy Ringlet and a few other species are adapted to living in rocky places, both high up in the mountains of the south and in low-lying, bare country in the far north beyond the Arctic Circle. The range of many butterflies is closely related to the distribution of the foodplant; the caterpillar of the Two-tailed Pasha, for example, feeds almost exclusively on the leaves of the Strawberry Tree (*Arbutus unedo*). A few, like the Small Heath, are very widespread wherever there are patches of grass, except at high altitudes.

The Red Admiral, Clouded Yellow, Painted Lady and a few other butterflies regularly migrate northwards in summer, but usually fail to overwinter in the north. At least one species, the Camberwell Beauty, crosses the North Sea from Scandinavia to Britain, and the Monarch probably starts its European migrations from the Canary Islands.

Watching and Identifying Butterflies

Observing butterflies, either with or without binoculars, can be as rewarding as bird-watching, and insect photography is a lot easier to succeed in than bird photography, though it is not without difficulties. Binoculars that can be focussed down to about 4 metres or less are best because it is usually necessary to get much closer to a butterfly than to a bird. A black or dark-coloured butterfly net is also useful; some species are very similar to others in colour-pattern, and it is often essential to capture a butterfly so that it can be examined and compared with the illustrations on pages 14-121.

To identify a butterfly, first match it for general appearance with the pictures opposite and then flip through the illustrations of its family in the main part of the book (pages 14-121). Having got fairly close, check the text to see whether the illustrated butterfly is generally found in the country and habitat where you caught it. If it is, look in the paragraph on identification to see whether other species resemble it and then look again at your specimen. Always examine both sides of the wings and check that the wing-span matches the range of measurements given in the text. You may have difficulties if you have caught a female Blue, many of which are, in fact, mostly brown and look much alike, so if you come across a mixture of small blue and not-so-blue butterflies examine them very carefully. A few European butterflies can only be identified by examining their internal structures under a microscope.

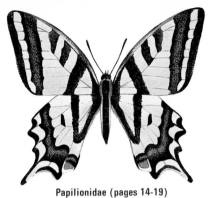

Papilionidae (pages 14-19)

Pieridae (pages 20-33)

Nymphalidae (pages 35-59)

Nymphalidae (pages 35-59)

Riodinidae (page 88)

Libytheidae (page 34)

Satyridae (pages 60-87)

Hesperiidae
(pages 114-21)

Lycaenidae (pages 88-113)

Lycaenidae (pages 88-113)

13

SWALLOWTAILS AND APOLLOS
Family Papilionidae

A worldwide group of just over 500 mostly large, colourful, fast-flying butterflies with 11 species in Europe. Most have tailed hind wings and all have three pairs of functional legs. Males differ little from the females in colour-pattern. The caterpillar has a retractable fleshy process behind the head. The chrysalis is usually attached to its foodplant by tail hooks and a girdle of silk.

Swallowtail

male

SWALLOWTAIL
Papilio machaon
60-98 mm. Flies between April and August in meadows and on flowery hillslopes in the lowlands and mountains up to about 2,000 metres. Occurs in North Africa, through most of Europe and across Asia as far as Japan. It is common in parts of continental Europe, but rare in Britain and found only in the marshy fens of East Anglia. There is usually one generation in the north but up to three in warmer parts of Europe.

The caterpillar feeds exclusively on the leaves of Umbellifers, chiefly Marsh Hog's Fennel (*Peucedanum palustre*) in England, but on other species elsewhere. The caterpillar is at first black and white and looks like a bird-dropping, but later becomes green, ringed with black and orange, and has an orange retractable process behind the head.

The chrysalis is usually attached to the foodplant and is the overwintering stage.

Identification The Corsican Swallowtail (*P. hospiton*) is the only other European butterfly resembling the Swallowtail, but it has a much more wavy edge to the dark band near the outer edge of the forewing.

14

Southern Swallowtail

male

Corsican Swallowtail

male

CORSICAN SWALLOWTAIL
Papilio hospiton
74-80 mm. Not found outside Sardinia and Corsica, where the butterfly is on the wing from May to July in the mountains up to about 1,200 metres. It is fairly rare and not widely distributed in the two islands.
The caterpillar feeds mainly on the leaves of Umbellifers, such as Giant Fennel (*Ferula communis*). It is green with a broad, broken band of black along the back, and rows of red spots on either side of the central line.
Identification The Swallowtail (*P. machaon*) is very similar to this species, but the black band near the edge of its forewing has almost straight edges.

SOUTHERN SWALLOWTAIL
Papilio alexanor
44-75 mm. The single yearly generation of this species flies between April and July, usually at moderate altitudes but as high as 1,200 metres. The butterflies often visit flowers, especially Thistles (*Cirsium* and *Carduus*). This is generally a rare species, except in southern France, and is very locally distributed. Found in southern Europe from France to Greece eastwards to China.
The caterpillar feeds on *Seseli montanum* and other Umbellifers. It is green, ringed with black and yellow.
The chrysalis overwinters.
Identification The Swallowtail (*P. machaon*) differs from this species in the colour of the wing bases.

15

Scarce Swallowtail

male

SCARCE SWALLOWTAIL
Iphiclides podalirius
65-84 mm. Now a protected species in parts of Europe, but widespread and quite common in places in North Africa and other parts of Europe northwards to the Baltic and across Asia to China. Specimens rarely reach England and Scandinavia, and never overwinter successfully. There are usually two generations each year flying in May and June and July and August. It is attracted to flowers and tree blossom in meadows, orchards and gardens, on grassy slopes, and along margins of woods; in places up to 1,800 metres.
The caterpillar is green, lined with yellow. It feeds on leaves of oak (*Quercus*), Blackthorn (*Prunus spinosa*) and other wild trees, as well as on cultivated cherries and other *Prunus* species.
The chrysalis is brown or yellow and is attached to the foodplant; it overwinters.
Identification No other European butterfly has a colour-pattern like that of the Scarce Swallowtail.

SOUTHERN FESTOON
Zerynthia polyxena
42-60 mm. The single generation of this fairly common species flies between March and June, seldom far above the ground, and it often visits flowers. Resident in rocky places up to 1,000 metres in southern Europe from southern France to Austria and south-eastwards to southern Russia. Not found in Spain or Portugal.
The caterpillar feeds on Birthwort (*Aristolochia clematitis*) and other species of the Aristolochiaceae family, a group of plants poisonous to mammals and birds.
The caterpillar varies in colour, but all have rows of brown and black hairy processes along the body.
The chrysalis also varies in colour, but all are usually speckled with black; it overwinters.
Identification The closly related Spanish Festoon (*Z.rumina*) differs in the presence of an extra red spot on the upper side towards the base of the forewing.

SPANISH FESTOON
Zerynthia rumina
38-50 mm. There is one flight of this rare species each year, usually between March and May. It prefers stony hillsides, especially near the sea, up to about 1,800 metres. Found only in North Africa, Spain, Portugal and southern France.

The caterpillar feeds on Birthwort (*Aristolochia*) species. It is orange, lined with black, and has rows of hairy, yellow processes along the body.

The chrysalis is grey and black, and overwinters.

Identification Only the Southern Festoon (*Z.polyxena*) is similar in colour-pattern but its upper side lacks a red spot towards the base of the forewing.

The bright colours of the Southern Festoon are a warning to enemies that this butterfly is distasteful.

Spanish Festoon
male

Southern Festoon
male

17

Apollo
male

APOLLO
Parnassius apollo
50-100 mm. Fairly common in the mountains of Europe (but not Britain) up to about 3,000 metres, and also at low elevations in Scandinavia and Finland. The single generation flies between May and September, usually in sunny places where the butterflies are attracted to flowers. The species is protected by law in many parts of Europe.

The caterpillar is black with grey-blue processes along the body, and orange spots along each side; it also has a Y-shaped retractable process behind the head. Stonecrops (*Sedum*) and, less often, Saxifrages (*Saxifraga*) are the caterpillar's foodplants. The Apollo overwinters as a young caterpillar inside the unbroken egg-shell. It often starts to feed in the spring before the snow has all melted, but only does so in full sunshine.

The chrysalis is brown, and usually hidden beneath a stone.

Identification The Small Apollo (*P. phoebus*) is similar in colour-pattern but usually lacks a black spot on the upper side near the rear edge of the forewing.

SMALL APOLLO
Parnassius phoebus
56-65 mm. Usually prefers damp, grassy mountainous areas, often near water and as high as 2,500 metres. Common in places in the Alps and mountains of Asia, Canada and the United States as far south as the southern limits of the Rockies.

The caterpillar feeds on the foliage of Saxifrages (*Saxifraga*), Stonecrops (*Sedum*) and related plants. It resembles the Apollo caterpillar, but has yellow spots on the sides.

The chrysalis also is similar to that of the Apollo and is hidden under a stone.

Identification The Apollo (*P.apollo*) is similarly coloured but has a conspicuous black spot on the upper side in the rear half of the forewing.

CLOUDED APOLLO
Parnassius mnemosyne
50-60 mm. A species from rather lower elevations than the previous two species, not usually found above 1,800 metres; often seen in areas where there are some bushes and trees. Inhabits central and northern Europe (but not Britain) as far east as central Asia. Flies usually between April and July in a single generation; rare in places, and protected by law in some countries.

The caterpillar feeds on the leaves of Corydalis (*Corydalis*), and is black, spotted with orange or yellow on the back. The young caterpillar overwinters inside the unbroken egg-shell.
The chrysalis is a dull yellow powdered with white, and is formed on the surface of the ground.
Identification This species differs from the other European Apollos in the absence of red spots on the wings.

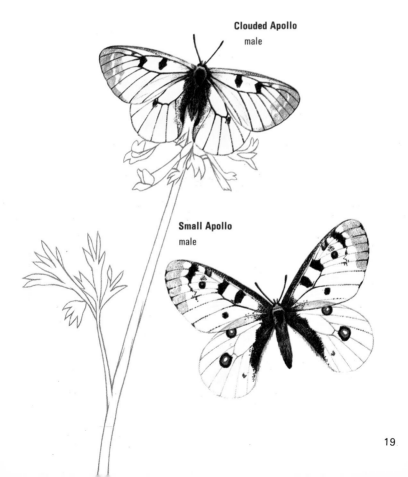

Clouded Apollo
male

Small Apollo
male

WHITES AND YELLOWS
Family Pieridae

A worldwide group of about 2,000 medium-sized species, with about 40 species in Europe. Males usually differ slightly from the females in colour-pattern. All six legs are functional. The caterpillars lack spines and are usually green in colour. Most feed on Legumes (Pea family) or Crucifers (Cabbage family) and some are agricultural pests. The chrysalis is attached head-upwards to the foodplant, or elsewhere, by tail hooks and a girdle of silk.

LARGE WHITE
Pieris brassicae
56-67 mm. A common butterfly in gardens, agricultural land and hill slopes up to 2,000 metres. There are two or three generations each year on the wing from April to August. Found in North Africa, in most of Europe and across Asia to the Himalayas. Often migrates in large numbers.

The caterpillar feeds in groups on Cabbage (*Brassica*) and other Crucifers, but also on garden Nasturtium (*Tropaeolum*). It is green striped with yellow, and mottled with black.

The chrysalis is attached either to the foodplant or to a nearby object. Autumn-generation chrysalids overwinter.

Identification Differs from the Small White (*Artogeia rapae*) in the larger size and the longer black marking at the outer edge of the forewing.

female

male

Large
White

male

The two Large Whites seen ▶ here end to end (the male above, female below) are mating. Courtship dances may precede mating.

Small White

male

male

Small White

female

SMALL WHITE
Artogeia rapae
46-54 mm. A common species in most of Europe, North Africa, northern Asia and North America, and a pest in farmlands of New Zealand and Australia. Found in gardens, meadows and agricultural land during most of the summer, with usually two generations in northern and up to four in southern Europe. Sometimes migrates in large numbers. Cabbage (*Brassica*) is a common food-plant, but wild Crucifers like Hedge Mustard (*Sisymbrium officinale*) are also eaten.

The caterpillar is green lined with yellow, and often chooses sheltered places on fences in which to change into a chrysalis.

The chrysalis usually matches the colour of its surroundings. The final generation of the year overwinters in this stage.

Identification Separable from the Large White (*Pieris brassicae*) by its size and the shorter black marking at the outer edge of the forewing. Two southern European whites resemble the Small White: the Mountain Small White (*P. ergane*), which lacks black spots on the underside of the wings, and the Southern Small White (*P. manni*), which has a larger black marking at the outer edge of the forewing.

GREEN-VEINED WHITE
Artogeia napi
39-51 mm. A migratory butterfly (less so than the Small White), but usually not a pest. Prefers meadows and hedgerows and often visits flowers. Except at high altitudes, there are usually two generations flying in May and June and in July and August. Found in North Africa, most of Europe, temperate Asia and western North America.

The caterpillar is pale green lined with dark green and yellow. It feeds mainly on Charlock (*Sinapis arvensis*) and other wild Crucifers.

The chrysalis, which is the overwintering stage, is usually secured to the foodplant but sometimes to sheds and fences.

Identification Separated from the similar Small White (*A.rapae*) by the dark green veins on the underside of the wings.

Green-veined Whites vary greatly in the extent of the dark markings.

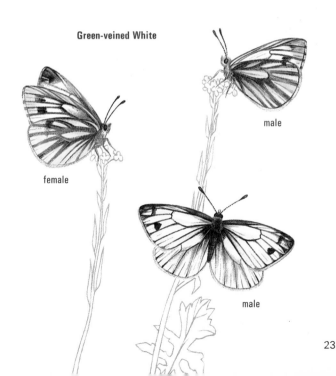

Green-veined White

male

female

male

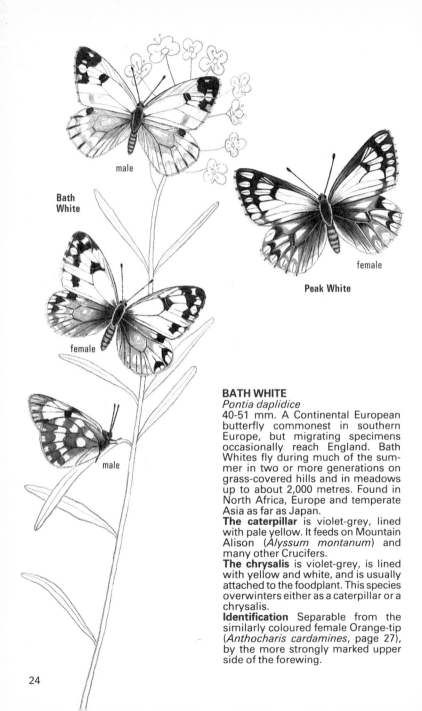

male

Bath White

female

male

female

Peak White

BATH WHITE
Pontia daplidice
40-51 mm. A Continental European butterfly commonest in southern Europe, but migrating specimens occasionally reach England. Bath Whites fly during much of the summer in two or more generations on grass-covered hills and in meadows up to about 2,000 metres. Found in North Africa, Europe and temperate Asia as far as Japan.

The caterpillar is violet-grey, lined with pale yellow. It feeds on Mountain Alison (*Alyssum montanum*) and many other Crucifers.

The chrysalis is violet-grey, is lined with yellow and white, and is usually attached to the foodplant. This species overwinters either as a caterpillar or a chrysalis.

Identification Separable from the similarly coloured female Orange-tip (*Anthocharis cardamines*, page 27), by the more strongly marked upper side of the forewing.

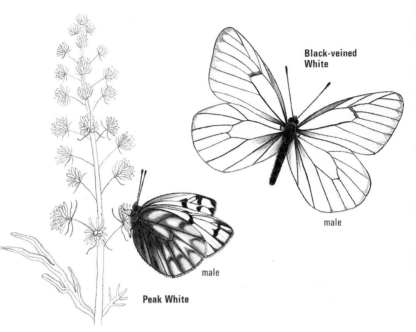

Black-veined
White

male

male

Peak White

PEAK WHITE
Pontia callidice
41-52 mm. Typically a mountain-summit butterfly, often flying close to the snow-line on mountains up to 3,000 metres high, usually as one generation in June and July. In warm years there may be two generations with a second flight in July and August. Found in the Pyrenees, Alps, Himalayas and in North America.
The caterpillar is like that of the Bath White but has two yellow and white lines along the back. It feeds on Mignonette (*Reseda lutea*), Cuckoo Flower (*Cardamine pratensis*) and many other Crucifers.
The chrysalis is either grey or green and hidden under stones. This species overwinters either as a chrysalis or a caterpillar.
Identification Probably most like the Green-veined White (*Artogeia napi*, page 23), but has a black spot in the centre of the forewing.

BLACK-VEINED WHITE
Aporia crataegi
57-67 mm. This buttterfly is common along hedgerows, in fields of Lucerne (*Medicago sativa*) and open country in some parts of Europe, North Africa and temperate Asia, and can be a pest in orchards. In Britain it is now extinct. The single generation flies in May, June and July.
The caterpillar feeds in groups on the foliage of Hawthorn (*Crataegus*), Blackthorn (*Prunus spinosa*) and Apple (*Malus*), and rests in a large silken nest. It is black, lined with orange, above, and grey, spotted with white, below. The partly grown caterpillars overwinter inside the nest.
The chrysalis varies in colour and is usually attached to a twig of the food-plant.
Identification The unspotted white wings of this species distinguish it from any other European butterfly. The female forewing is almost transparent.

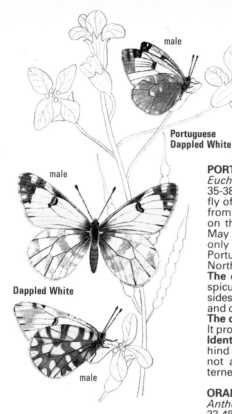

male

Portuguese
Dappled White

male

Dappled White

male

PORTUGUESE DAPPLED WHITE
Euchloe tagis
35-38 mm. This is a fast-flying butterfly of rocky and mostly hilly country, from sea-level to 1,000 metres, and is on the wing between February and May in a single generation. Found only in a few places in southern Portugal, Spain and France, and in North Africa.

The caterpillar is green with a conspicuous white-edged red line on the sides, and feeds on Candytufts (*Iberis*) and other Crucifers.

The chrysalis is mainly bluish-brown; It probably overwinters.

Identification The front edge of the hind wing of this species is rounded, not angled as in the similarly patterned Dappled White (*E.ausonia*).

ORANGE-TIP
Anthocharis cardamines
33-48 mm. The butterflies of the single yearly generation usually emerge between March and July. They fly along hedgerows and in meadows, often near woods, and are frequently attracted to flowers. Found in most of Europe as far north as the Arctic Circle and across Asia to Japan.

The caterpillar is green with black spots and white lines. It feeds on Cuckoo Flower (*Cardamine pratensis*) and other Crucifers and eventually changes into a chrysalis on or near the foodplant.

The chrysalis, which overwinters, can be green, yellow, or brown.

Identification The males are easily separable from other orange-tipped species in Europe. The females are like the female Dappled White (*Euchloe ausonia*) in colour-pattern, but the grey apical area under the forewing is not lined with green along the veins.

DAPPLED WHITE
Euchloe ausonia
39-48 mm. Flies in June and July in the mountains from 1,500 to 2,000 metres in a single generation, but has two generations at low elevations on the wing between March and June. Found in southern and central Europe, temperate Asia and in the Rockies of Canada and the United States.

The caterpillar has blue and white stripes and feeds on Wild Radish (*Raphanus raphanistrum*), Rockcress (*Arabis*) and other Crucifers.

The chrysalis is brown with dark brown markings; it overwinters.

Identification The front edge of the hind wing is unusual in being distinctly angled, not evenly rounded, a character that separates this butterfly from the Portuguese Dappled White (*E.tagis*) and other Whites with similar colour-patterns.

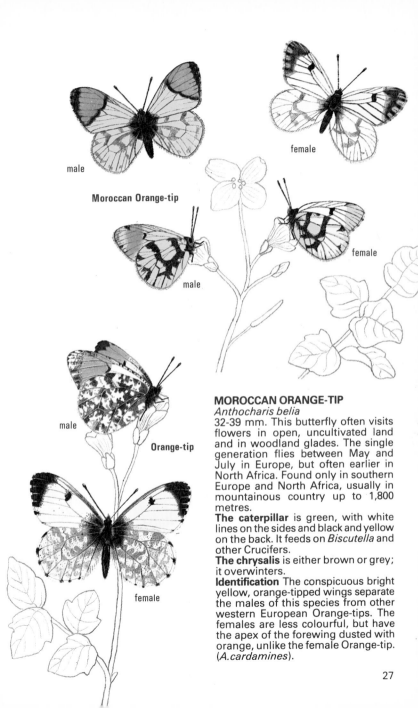

male

female

Moroccan Orange-tip

female

male

male

Orange-tip

female

MOROCCAN ORANGE-TIP
Anthocharis belia
32-39 mm. This butterfly often visits flowers in open, uncultivated land and in woodland glades. The single generation flies between May and July in Europe, but often earlier in North Africa. Found only in southern Europe and North Africa, usually in mountainous country up to 1,800 metres.

The caterpillar is green, with white lines on the sides and black and yellow on the back. It feeds on *Biscutella* and other Crucifers.

The chrysalis is either brown or grey; it overwinters.

Identification The conspicuous bright yellow, orange-tipped wings separate the males of this species from other western European Orange-tips. The females are less colourful, but have the apex of the forewing dusted with orange, unlike the female Orange-tip. (*A.cardamines*).

27

male

male

Northern Clouded Yellow

female

male

male

Pale Arctic Clouded Yellow

female

NORTHERN CLOUDED YELLOW
Colias hecla
36-41 mm. The yearly generation usually flies at the end of June and in July on heaths and open grassland up to about 1,000 metres, but only at low elevations in the extreme north. Found only north of the Arctic Circle in Europe, Asia, Greenland, Alaska and Canada.
The caterpillar has been recorded feeding on Alpine Milk Vetch (*Astragalus alpinus*). It probably overwinters twice before becoming full grown and changing into a chrysalis.
The chrysalis is not known.
Identification Much more orange in colour than the Clouded Yellow (*C. crocea*, page 30), and Pale Clouded Yellow (*C.hyale*, page 31), and the wings appear red when viewed from the side at an oblique angle.

PALE ARCTIC CLOUDED YELLOW
Colias nastes
40-45 mm. A solely Arctic species in Europe and present also in northern Asia, North America and Greenland. A fast-flying butterfly, on the wing in June and July in a single generation on moorland above 300 metres.
The caterpillar overwinters full grown, and feeds on Alpine Milk Vetch (*Astragalus alpinus*).
The chrysalis is not known.
Identification Similar to the Clouded Yellow (*C.crocea*, page 30) in colour-pattern, but the latter is not an Arctic species and other Arctic Clouded Yellows are more yellowish or orange in colour.

*Berger's Clouded Yellow (*Colias australis*) is one of several European 'Yellows'. All have a similar underside colour-pattern.*

male

Mountain
Clouded
Yellow

male

female

MOUNTAIN CLOUDED YELLOW
Colias phicomone
39-47 mm. An alpine butterfly found in meadows and on grass slopes up to 2,400 metres. Restricted to the Alps and Pyrenees. There is usually one generation, flying in July and August, but sometimes two, with a second flight in late August and September.
The caterpillar is green mottled with black, and has a white stripe on the sides. It feeds on various kinds of Vetches, including *Vicia* and *Coronilla*, Lucerne (*Medicago sativa*) and other Legumes. Overwintering caterpillars start to feed again early in the spring. **The chrysalis** is green, striped with yellow on the sides.
Identification This is the only western European Clouded Yellow living in mountainous regions that has grey-ish-yellow wings.

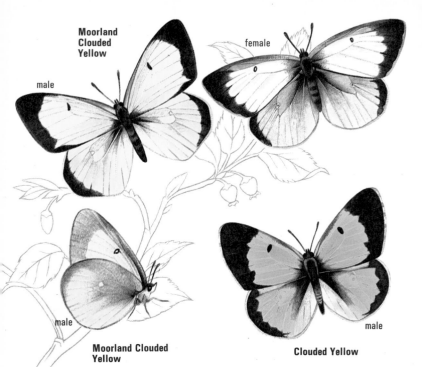

Moorland Clouded Yellow
male
female
male
Moorland Clouded Yellow
male
Clouded Yellow

MOORLAND CLOUDED YELLOW
Colias palaeno
38-42 mm. A locally common butterfly, but decreasing in numbers following drainage of marshes and wet moors and meadows where the caterpillar's foodplant grows. Flies in June, July and August in a single generation, often near woods from sea-level to 2,500 metres. Found in France and northern Europe (but not Britain) across Asia to Japan, and also in North America.
The caterpillar is green, striped with yellow and black, and feeds on Northern Bilberry (*Vaccinium uliginosum*) and other species of *Vaccinium*. It overwinters.
The chrysalis is green in colour.
Identification Separated from other Clouded Yellows by the greenish-white or yellow colour of the wings and the unspotted, dark brown marginal bands.

CLOUDED YELLOW
Colias crocea
47-61 mm. Migrates northwards during the summer, but a year-long resident in southern Europe, south-western Asia and North Africa. Flies from early spring until October in a succession of generations. Found in meadows up to about 1,500 metres, and often common in fields of Lucerne (*Medicago sativa*) and Clover (*Trifolium*).
The caterpillar is green, with a line of yellow and red, and a row of black spots on the side. It feeds on Clovers and Lucerne and other Legumes and changes into a chrysalis on the foodplant. The last generation of the year overwinters in the caterpillar stage.
The chrysalis is green, marked with yellow, bláck and brown.
Identification Differs from the Pale Clouded Yellow (*C.hyale*) in the absence of a yellow apical band on the male forewing.

PALE CLOUDED YELLOW
Colias hyale

44-54 mm. Less of a southern species than the Clouded Yellow. Resident in southern and central Europe, migrating in warm years to Britain and Scandinavia. Occurs also in temperate western and central Asia. There are two generations each year, the first flying in May and June, the second in August and September. Often visits fields of Lucerne (*Medicago sativa*) and Clover (*Trifolium*), but also found in grassy country up to about 2,000 metres.

The caterpillar feeds on Vetches (*Hippocrepis* and *Coronilla*), Lucerne, Clovers and other Legumes. It is green, striped with white, orange and yellow. Caterpillars of the second generation overwinter.

The chrysalis is yellow or green, marked with brown and black.

Identification Difficult to separate from Berger's Clouded Yellow (*C. australis*, see photograph on page 29), although the caterpillars are differently coloured and easy to identify. Fairly easily distinguished from the Clouded Yellow (*C.crocea*).

male

Clouded Yellow

female

male

Pale Clouded Yellow

male

female

31

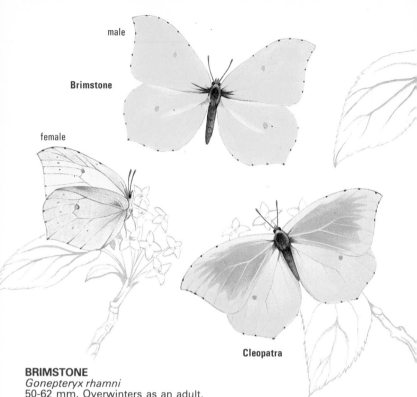

male

Brimstone

female

Cleopatra

BRIMSTONE
Gonepteryx rhamni
50-62 mm. Overwinters as an adult, and one of the first butterflies to appear in the spring. Flies on heaths, and along hedges and the edges of woods during June and July. Found in most of Europe, except the Arctic and Scotland, at elevations up to 2,000 metres.

The caterpillar feeds on Buckthorn (*Rhamnus catharticus*) and, less often, on Alder Buckthorn (*Frangula alnus*). It is green, spotted with black and striped with darker green and white.

The chrysalis is green and brown, and secured to the stems of plants close to the ground.

Identification The males are easily distinguished from male Cleopatra butterflies (*G.cleopatra*) by the yellow or greenish-white forewings; the females are identified mainly by the absence of an orange area on the underside of the forewing.

CLEOPATRA
Gonepteryx cleopatra
50-60 mm. Flies from May onwards in open woods or scrubland, often on mountain slopes up to 2,000 metres. Found only in southern Europe and western Asia. There is usually one generation in Europe but more than one in Asia.

The caterpillar feeds mainly on species of *Rhamnus*. It is similar to the caterpillar of the Brimstone but is more bluish in colour.

The chrysalis is not known.

Identification The males differ from the Brimstone (*G.rhamni*) chiefly in the much more orange colour of the upper side of the forewing; the female differs most noticeably on the underside of the forewing, where there is a faint orange area near the base.

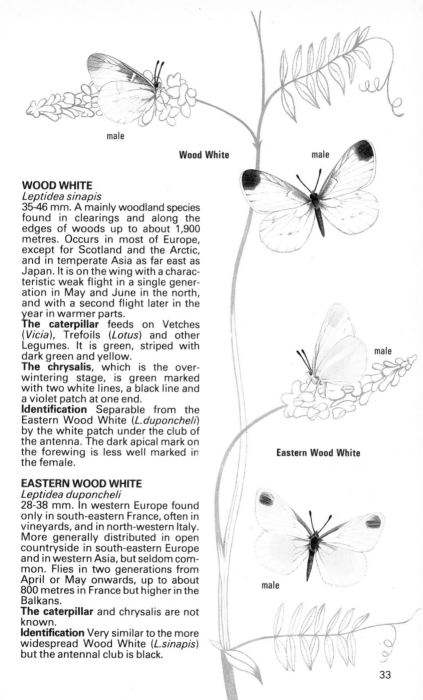

male

Wood White

male

male

Eastern Wood White

male

WOOD WHITE
Leptidea sinapis
35-46 mm. A mainly woodland species found in clearings and along the edges of woods up to about 1,900 metres. Occurs in most of Europe, except for Scotland and the Arctic, and in temperate Asia as far east as Japan. It is on the wing with a characteristic weak flight in a single generation in May and June in the north, and with a second flight later in the year in warmer parts.
The caterpillar feeds on Vetches (*Vicia*), Trefoils (*Lotus*) and other Legumes. It is green, striped with dark green and yellow.
The chrysalis, which is the overwintering stage, is green marked with two white lines, a black line and a violet patch at one end.
Identification Separable from the Eastern Wood White (*L.duponcheli*) by the white patch under the club of the antenna. The dark apical mark on the forewing is less well marked in the female.

EASTERN WOOD WHITE
Leptidea duponcheli
28-38 mm. In western Europe found only in south-eastern France, often in vineyards, and in north-western Italy. More generally distributed in open countryside in south-eastern Europe and in western Asia, but seldom common. Flies in two generations from April or May onwards, up to about 800 metres in France but higher in the Balkans.
The caterpillar and chrysalis are not known.
Identification Very similar to the more widespread Wood White (*L.sinapis*) but the antennal club is black.

33

Monarch

Nettle-tree
Butterfly

SNOUT BUTTERFLIES
Family Libytheidae

A small but worldwide group of
medium-sized species confined
to the tropics of Africa, Asia
and Australasia, except for one
European species. Many are
migratory in habit. Females
have well-developed forelegs;
males have reduced forelegs, as
in the closely related Family
Nymphalidae. Both sexes
have a toothed margin to the
forewing and most have long,
beak-like palps. The chrysalis is
suspended from hooks at the
tail end.

NETTLE-TREE BUTTERFLY
Libythea celtis
36-42 mm. Found only where there
are Nettle-trees (*Celtis australis*) and
restricted to North Africa, southern
Europe up to about 800 metres, and
across Asia to Japan. Flies in June,
July and August in a single generation, but also in early spring when
overwintering butterflies reappear.
The caterpillar is brown or green,
striped with white and black. It feeds
on Nettle-tree foliage but also sometimes on cultivated Cherry (*Prunus
cerasus*).
The chrysalis is green in colour.
Identification Not likely to be confused
with any other European butterfly.

MONARCHS, TIGERS
AND CROWS
Family Danaidae

Chiefly a tropical Asian and
African group of mostly large
species, but also represented in
North, Central and South
America. The forelegs of both
sexes are greatly reduced, as in
the closely related Nymphalidae.
The caterpillars, which lack
spines, feed mainly on species
of the poisonous plant families
Asclepiadaceae (Milkweeds) and
Apocyanaceae (Dogbane and
others), and the plant poisons
are passed on to the adult
butterflies. Insect-eating
birds learn to associate the
bright colours and patterns of
Danaids with their unpleasant
taste and leave them alone. The
chrysalids hang upside-down from
hooks at the tail end, and are
often marked with shiny gold or
silver spots.

MONARCH
Danaus plexippus
75-100 mm. Typically a butterfly of flowery meadows in open or wooded country. Migrates northwards in North America in a series of generations in the spring and summer and returns in the autumn. Some butterflies reach overwintering sites far to the south in California and Florida, and in Mexico where millions of specimens congregate. The migratory habit of the Monarch probably accounts for the immense range that includes North and South America, and parts of South-east Asia eastwards to Australia and New Zealand, but not continental Asia or Africa, although the Monarch has reached the Canaries and Azores. A few specimens are found in Britain and western Europe, but the origin of these is not known.
The caterpillar feeds almost exclusively on Milkweeds (Asclepiadaceae), a poisonous group of plants. It is ringed with black, white and yellow, and has two black, fleshy processes behind the head and two near the rear end of the body. Caterpillars and adults store plant poisons and are avoided by insect-eating birds.
The chrysalis is a shiny green, marked with black and metallic gold.
Identification No other butterfly found in Europe has a colour-pattern resembling that of the Monarch. Females are slightly paler in colour than the males.

ADMIRALS, EMPERORS, VANESSIDS AND FRITILLARIES
Family Nymphalidae

A worldwide group of several thousand medium-sized species, with about 70 representatives in Europe. All the species have reduced forelegs and most are colourful, strongly flying butterflies. The upper-side colour-pattern usually differs from that of the underside, but males and females resemble each other fairly closely. The caterpillars are generally covered with spines. The chrysalids are often ornamented with shiny gold or silver markings, and are suspended from hooks at the tail end.

TWO-TAILED PASHA
Charaxes jasius
76-85 mm. In Europe confined to the Mediterranean coast, in dry places up to about 1,000 metres and where there are Strawberry Trees (*Arbutus unedo*). Found also in North Africa, and in much of tropical Africa. A strongly flying species often high up in the trees, but can also be seen on the ground feeding on decaying animal matter and fruit. There are two generations in Europe, on the wing between May and September.
The caterpillar usually feeds on the Strawberry Tree but also sometimes on Poplar (*Populus*). It is green, striped with yellow on the sides, and has two green and blue spots on the back and four red horns on the head. Caterpillars of the second generation hibernate in Europe but there is no long resting stage in the tropics.
The chrysalis is green, marked with red.
Identification Both upper and under sides of this butterfly are distinctive.

Two-tailed
Pasha

male

Lesser
Purple
Emperor

male

Purple
Emperor

male

male

female

PURPLE EMPEROR
Apatura iris

64-80 mm. Males usually fly around the upper branches of Oak trees (*Quercus*), but may be attracted to rotting animal material and damp patches on the ground. Fairly common in July and August up to about 1,500 metres in much of Europe, including Britain, but not in Sweden or Norway.

The caterpillar, which overwinters, is green, marked with yellow and white, and has two long horns on the head. It feeds mostly on Sallows (*Salix*), resting along the middle of a leaf on a layer of silk.

The chrysalis is green, striped with dark green, and is attached to a twig.

Identification Separated from the Lesser Purple Emperor (*A.ilia*) by details of the colour-pattern.

36

LESSER PURPLE EMPEROR
Apatura ilia
64-70 mm. A rather scarce butterfly of open woodlands, up to about 1,500 metres. On the wing between April and June and again in August and September, but with only one generation in the north and the Alps. Found in southern and central Europe (not Britain or Scandinavia) and in temperate Asia as far east as Japan.

The caterpillar is green, spotted and striped with yellow, and has two processes on the head. It feeds mainly on Black Poplar (*Populus nigra*) and other Poplars, but probably also on Willow (*Salix*) and other trees. The caterpillar overwinters.

The chrysalis is greenish-white, marked with yellow.

Identification Separated from the Purple Emperor (*A. iris*) by the orange margin around the dark spot near the edge of the upper side of the forewing.

POPLAR ADMIRAL
Limenitis populi
70-80 mm. Common in woodland clearings up to about 1,500 metres in some areas but rare and local in others. The male usually flies high up in the trees, but may descend to feed on rotting animal matter and fruit. Appears in June and July in a single flight. Found in central Europe as far north as the Arctic Circle, but not in Britain.

The caterpillar is mostly green, with two rows of fleshy processes along the back, and four shiny patches on the middle of the back. It feeds on Aspen (*Populus tremula*) and other Poplars (*Populus*), and overwinters in a rolled dead leaf.

The chrysalis is dull yellow, marked with brown and black, and is concealed in a rolled leaf of the foodplant.

Identification The colour-pattern of the upper side is unlike that of any other European butterfly.

Poplar Admiral

male

male

SOUTHERN WHITE ADMIRAL
Limenitis reducta
42-48 mm. Widespread and locally common near woods and in woodland glades up to about 1,000 metres. Flies throughout the summer in two or three generations, except in the north and at high elevations in the south where there is only one flight each year. Found in southern and central Europe and in western Asia.

The caterpillar is green, striped with white, and has two rows of red spines along the body. It feeds on Honeysuckle (*Lonicera*), spinning a web under a leaf. Caterpillars of the autumn generation overwinter.

The chrysalis is grey, with shiny silvery markings, and is attached to the foodplant.

Identification Unlike the White Admiral (*Ladoga camilla*), this species has only one row of black spots on the underside along the margin of the hind wing.

WHITE ADMIRAL
Ladoga camilla
52-60 mm. A woodland species often attracted to Bramble (*Rubus*) flowers and decaying animal matter. Fairly common in a single flight during June and July up to 1,500 metres in most of Europe, except for the extreme south and north, and also found in temperate Asia as far east as Japan.

The caterpillar is green, striped with purple and white, and when young, attaches droppings to its body as camouflage. It feeds on Honeysuckle (*Lonicera*) and overwinters on the foodplant.

The chrysalis is green with brown and shiny silvery marks, and looks like a dew-covered dead leaf.

Identification Similar to the Southern White Admiral (*Limenitis reducta*), but has two rows of black spots near the margin of the hind wing on the underside.

male

Southern White Admiral

male

male

White Admiral

male

Camberwell
Beauty

male

Large
Tortoiseshell

male

CAMBERWELL BEAUTY
Nymphalis antiopa
60-73 mm. An elegant, strongly flying, migratory butterfly of open woodlands, particularly in hilly areas up to about 1,500 metres. Fond of feeding on rotting fruit and animal matter. The single yearly flight appears in June and July and continues until the autumn, when the survivors hibernate until early the following year. Found in North America and temperate Asia and in most of Europe, but in Britain only as a rare migrant from Scandinavia.
The caterpillar is black with red markings and has numerous hairy spines. It feeds on Sallows (*Salix*) and other trees.
The chrysalis is spiny, and is brown, marked with black and orange. It is attached to a twig of the foodplant.
Identification The colour-pattern is unlike that of any other butterfly in the world.

LARGE TORTOISESHELL
Nymphalis polychloros
54-66 mm. Usually found near woods, along old hedgerows, or in orchards where rotting fruit proves attractive. The butterflies emerge in July and August, then hibernate and fly again in the spring. Found in eastern England, most of continental Europe from sea-level to 1,300 metres, North Africa and western Asia.
The caterpillar is black, striped with brownish-orange, and has numerous yellow spines. It feeds in a group on Elm (*Ulmus*), Sallow (*Salix*) and other trees.
The chrysalis is reddish-brown, marked with green and shiny silvery spots, and is formed in a crevice of the bark.
Identification Separated from the Small Tortoiseshell (*Aglais urticae*, page 41) by its size and the colour-pattern of the hind wing.

male

male

Peacock

Red Admiral

male

male

PEACOCK
Inachis io

56-68 mm. Regularly visits *Buddleia* in gardens and attracted to Knap-weeds (*Centaurea*) and other flowers. The main flight is from June onwards, the survivors overwintering until the following spring to produce the next year's generation. Generally common in Europe up to about 1,500 metres, except in Arctic Scandinavia, and across Asia to Japan. The unusual colour-pattern of the upper side possibly scares away small birds when the butterfly suddenly opens its wings to reveal eye-spots.

The caterpillar feeds in a group on the young leaves of Nettles (*Urtica*). It is black, spotted with white, and has numerous branched, black spines.

The chrysalis varies in colour, but is commonly greenish-yellow, mottled with brown or black, and has a gold lustre. It is often suspended from a twig of a nearby bush.

Identification The colour-pattern of this butterfly is unique.

RED ADMIRAL
Vanessa atalanta

56-68 mm. A generally common species of meadows, hedgerows, orchards and gardens, and attracted to flowers and rotten fruit. Possibly overwinters as an adult in Britain, but usually first appears in May as a migrant from the south and produces a main flight in late summer together with further migrants. Found in much of Europe and across Asia to India, in North Africa, and in North and Central America.

The caterpillar is mainly black, with brown and yellow spines. It feeds alone, in a web, usually on Nettles (*Urtica*).

The chrysalis is attached to the web spun by the caterpillar. It is grey-brown, with shiny golden spots.

Identification No other European butterfly has a colour-pattern like that of the Red Admiral.

male

Painted
Lady

male

male

Small Tortoiseshell

PAINTED LADY
Cynthia cardui
54-65 mm. Sometimes common in northern Europe and even in Iceland as a migrant, but overwinters probably only in warmer regions. Flies in gardens, often visiting *Buddleia* flowers, and up to 3,000 metres in open country and woodland clearings. Occurs throughout the year in the tropics but has only two generations in the north. Almost worldwide in distribution but not known in South America.
The caterpillar feeds alone in a web under leaves of Thistles (*Carduus* and *Cirsium*), Nettles (*Urtica*) and other plants. It is mainly black, and is covered with yellow or yellow and black spines.
The chrysalis is grey, often with shiny gold markings. It is usually suspended under a leaf.
Identification Unlike any other European butterfly in colour-pattern.

SMALL TORTOISESHELL
Aglais urticae
44-52 mm. One of the most abundant European butterflies wherever there are flowers, and a common visitor to Ice-plant (*Sedum*) and *Buddleia* flowers. This species does migrate, but not in great numbers. It overwinters as an adult butterfly and can be seen as early as March, flying until September or October in two or more generations. Found throughout Europe and temperate Asia to Japan from sea-level to 3,500 metres.

male

The caterpillar lives with others in a large web on Nettles (*Urtica*). It is usually black above and greenish below, with several rows of black and yellow spines.
The chrysalis is formed under fence rails or in similar protected places. It is grey, with shiny, golden spots.
Identification Best separated from the Large Tortoiseshell (*Nymphalis polychloros*, page 39) by the uniformly black base to the hind wing.

COMMA
Polygonia c-album
44-54 mm. Butterflies of both the first (June and July) and second (August) generations may overwinter and appear again in March and April. Found in orchards, gardens and along hedgerows and woods in most of Europe (but not Ireland or northern Britain), and as far east as Japan. Often attracted to *Buddleia* and Ice-plant (*Sedum*) flowers.

The caterpillar lives alone in a small web under a leaf, usually on Nettles (*Urtica*). It is black, marked with yellow and white, and is covered with white or yellow spines.

The chrysalis hangs from a twig of the foodplant. It is usually dull pink in colour, marked with green and black, and has several shiny, silver spots on the back.

Identification Differs from the Southern Comma (*P. egea*) in the distinctly comma-like white marking under the hind wing.

SOUTHERN COMMA
Polygonia egea
44-46 mm. On the wing in two generations during May and June and in August and September, but also in early spring when the overwintering autumn butterflies fly again. Can be common up to 1,200 metres in dry, stony places, pastures and sometimes gardens. Found only in southern Europe and western Asia.

The caterpillar feeds mainly on Pellitory (*Parietaria*), but also on Nettles (*Urtica*). It is greyish-green or blue, spotted with black, ringed with black and yellow, and has several rows of mostly yellow spines along the body.

The chrysalis is brownish-yellow, with three rows of short spines along the back.

Identification The white mark on the underside of the hind wing is Y-shaped rather than comma-shaped.

male

Comma

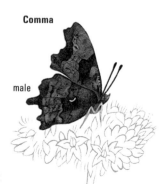

male

Southern Comma

The colour of the spring-generation European Map Butterfly contrasts with the black and white (or yellow) of the summer generation.

MAP BUTTERFLY
Araschnia levana

32-40 mm. The normally two generations of this woodland species are very different from each other. Butterflies of the first generation (April to early July) are orange and black, those of the second generation (July and August) black and white. Generally a lowland species, but sometimes occurs up to about 1,000 metres. Found fairly commonly in France and Germany, but not in Britain nor in most of southern Europe or Scandinavia. Also occurs in Japan and much of temperate Asia.

The caterpillar feeds on Nettles (*Urtica*), at first in a group but later alone. It is black or brown, with many long yellow and black spines.

The chrysalis, the overwintering stage, is green, sometimes with shiny, silvery patches.

Identification Both the upper side and map-like underside are distinctively patterned, and separate this butterfly from all other European species.

male
(first
generation)

male
(first
generation)

Map Butterfly

male
(second
generation)

43

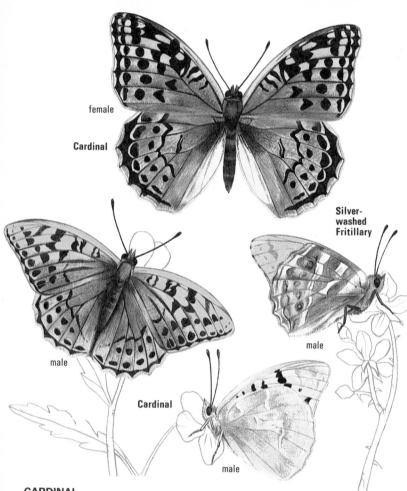

female
Cardinal

Silver-washed Fritillary

male

male

Cardinal

male

CARDINAL
Pandoriana pandora
66-80 mm. A fast-flying species common in Europe south of the Alps, in parts of western Asia as far east as Pakistan, and in North Africa. Rarely migrates to Britain. On the wing in June and July in Europe, but in two generations between May and September in the south of its range. Visits flowers in meadows and on heaths, usually near woods, up to 1,800 metres in the Atlas mountains but less high in the Alps.

The caterpillar, which overwinters, is brown, spotted with white, and has rows of yellow and grey spines along the body. It feeds on Wild Pansy (*Viola tricolor*) and other species of *Viola*.
The chrysalis is brown or grey, with shiny, gold spots.
Identification Separated from the more widespread Silver-washed Fritillary (*Argynnis paphia*) by the red areas on the underside of the forewing.

SILVER-WASHED FRITILLARY
Argynnis paphia
56-74 mm. Flies in or near woods between June and September in a single yearly generation, and can be quite common up to about 1,000 metres. Often visits Bramble (*Rubus*) flowers. Found in most of Europe, including Britain, but not in Arctic Scandinavia.
The caterpillar feeds chiefly on Dog Violet (*Viola riviniana*), but in the first few months of its life it overwinters in the crevices of the bark of Oaks (*Quercus*) and Pines (*Pinus*).
The chrysalis is brown, with shiny, gold spots, and is formed on or near the foodplant.
Identification Most like the Cardinal (*Pandoriana pandora*), but the forewing is brownish- or greenish-yellow below, not red.

DARK GREEN FRITILLARY
Mesoacidalia aglaja
48-65 mm. Inhabits wooded areas, but also heaths and hillsides with shrubs. Flies from June to August in a single generation, usually at low elevations in the north, but generally at high elevations in the south and up to 2,000 metres in North Africa. Widely distributed in Europe, except in the Arctic, and in temperate Asia eastwards to Japan.
The caterpillar feeds usually on Violets (*Viola*). It hibernates on the foodplant soon after hatching. When full-grown it is black and red, spotted with white and orange, and has numerous black spines along the body.
The chrysalis is brown, marked with black, and is protected by a cocoon of leaves and silk attached to the foodplant or close by.
Identification Like the High Brown Fritillary (*Fabriciana adippe*, page 46) in colour-pattern, but lacks a row of round spots near the outer edge of the hind wing on the underside.

female

Dark Green
Fritillary

Silver-washed
Fritillary

male

male

High Brown Fritillary

male

Niobe Fritillary

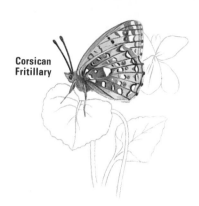

Corsican Fritillary

HIGH BROWN FRITILLARY
Fabriciana adippe
50-64 mm. The single flight of this species extends from June to August. The butterflies are equally at home in woodland clearings and in more open country, from sea-level to about 2,000 metres. Fairly local in Britain, but quite common in parts of continental Europe, except for northern Scandinavia. Found also in North Africa and temperate Asia, including Japan.
The caterpillar can be seen inside its egg-shell in the autumn, but does not hatch out until the spring. It feeds on Violets (*Viola*), and when full-grown is brown, with red or pink spines.
The chrysalis is brown, with shiny, golden-green spots. It is suspended inside a tent of silk and leaves on the foodplant.
Identification Separable from the Dark Green Fritillary (*Mesoacidalia aglaja*, page 45) by the row of round spots on the underside near the margin of the hind wing.

NIOBE FRITILLARY
Fabriciana niobe
46-60 mm. Not known in Britain or northern Scandinavia, but otherwise widely distributed in Europe and western Asia. Locally common in a single flight during June, July and August in grassy and shrubby country up to 2,000 metres and on coastal sand-dunes in Holland and Belgium. Overwinters as an unhatched caterpillar inside the egg-shell.
The caterpillar usually feeds on Violets (*Viola*), and when full-grown is brown, striped with black and white, and is covered with pink spines.
The chrysalis is olive-green, with shiny, silver spots.
Identification Differs from the similar High Brown Fritillary (*F.adippe*) mainly on the underside of the hind wing, where there is usually a black-centred yellow spot in the cell.

CORSICAN FRITILLARY
Fabriciana elisa
36-42 mm. Locally common in open woodlands and heaths on the Mediterranean islands of Sardinia and Corsica. Not known elsewhere. The butterflies are on the wing in June and July and are generally confined to the mountains up to 1,500 metres.
The caterpillar probably feeds on Violets (*Viola*).
The chrysalis is not known.
Identification Unlikely to be confused with any other Fritillary in Corsica or Sardinia.

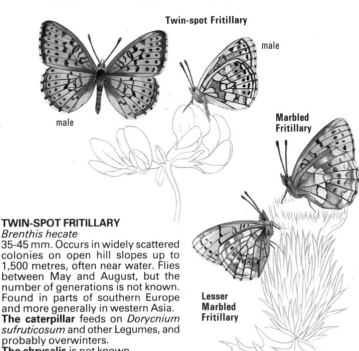

Twin-spot Fritillary

male

male

Marbled Fritillary

Lesser Marbled Fritillary

TWIN-SPOT FRITILLARY
Brenthis hecate
35-45 mm. Occurs in widely scattered colonies on open hill slopes up to 1,500 metres, often near water. Flies between May and August, but the number of generations is not known. Found in parts of southern Europe and more generally in western Asia.
The caterpillar feeds on *Dorycnium sufruticosum* and other Legumes, and probably overwinters.
The chrysalis is not known.
Identification Similar to several other Fritillaries, but distinguished by the double row of black spots on the underside of the hind wing.

MARBLED FRITILLARY
Brenthis daphne
42-54 mm. Flies during June and July in dry woodland meadows up to 1,500 metres, often visiting Bramble (*Rubus*) flowers. Common in some Swiss localities but generally uncommon in Europe. The range includes southern Europe and much of temperate Asia, including Japan.
The caterpillar, which overwinters, is brown, striped with white and yellow, and has numerous yellow spines along the body. It feeds on Violets (*Viola*), Raspberry and Bramble.
The chrysalis is yellow-grey, with red and shiny, gold spots.
Identification Much like the Lesser Marbled Fritillary (*B.ino*) but with a row of black dashes, not spots, near the margin of the hind wing on the upper side.

LESSER MARBLED FRITILLARY
Brenthis ino
34-40 mm. Flies slowly and close to the ground, often visiting Alpine Ragwort (*Senecio nemorensis*), Thistles (*Carduus* and *Cirsium*) and other flowers in marshy moors and woodland meadows. The single yearly flight is during June, July and August. Locally common in central and northern Europe (not Britain), up to 1,500 metres, and across Asia to Japan.
The caterpillar is pale yellow, marked with brown, and is covered with yellow spines. It feeds on Great Burnet (*Sanguisorba officinalis*), Meadowsweet (*Filipendula ulmaria*) and other plants. Hibernation takes place either as a partly grown caterpillar or in the egg stage.
The chrysalis is yellow-brown, with two rows of yellow knobs on the back.
Identification See the Marbled Fritillary (*B.daphne*).

47

QUEEN OF SPAIN FRITILLARY
Issoria lathonia
36-48 mm. A rare migrant in Britain and northern Scandinavia, but often common in continental Europe, North Africa and temperate Asia in rough sandy country, regularly visiting Scabious (*Succisa*) and other flowers. The single northern generation flies in May and June, but there are up to three generations in the south between February and October. Migrants to the north may breed and produce another generation, but the offspring never overwinter successfully.

The caterpillar is black, marked with white, and has many black and brown spines. It feeds on Violets (*Viola*). Autumn caterpillars overwinter.

The chrysalis is greenish-brown, with shiny, gold spots and other markings, and is formed inside a tent of leaves and silk.

Identification The wing shape and underside colour-pattern are distinctive.

MOUNTAIN FRITILLARY
Boloria napaea
32-42 mm. Fairly common in July and August high in the mountains, from the edge of the tree zone upwards to about 3,000 metres in the Alps, often in damp areas. Found in the Pyrenees, Alps, Scandinavia, northern Asia and in north-western North America.

The caterpillar feeds on species of *Polygonum*, including Alpine Bistort (*P. viviparum*), and overwinters twice before changing into a chrysalis.

The chrysalis is not known.

Identification Similar to the Cranberry Fritillary (*B. aquilonaris*), but the black markings on the underside are absent or nearly so. The Shepherd's Fritillary (*B. pales*, not illustrated) is similar to the Mountain Fritillary but is less brightly coloured on the underside of the hind wing. Generally found at higher elevations than the Mountain Fritillary.

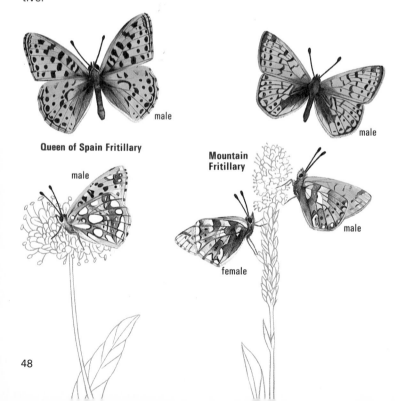

Queen of Spain Fritillary

male

male

Mountain Fritillary

male

male

female

CRANBERRY FRITILLARY
Boloria aquilonaris
32-40 mm. A butterfly of wet moors and bogs, where it flies in June and early July. Found up to 1,500 metres in northern Europe (including the Arctic but not Britain), in parts of central Europe as far south as the Alps, and probably in Asia. Locally quite common.

The caterpillar feeds on Cranberry (*Vaccinium oxycoccus*), and over-winters amongst moss at the foot of the foodplant.

The chrysalis is not known.

Identification Separated from the Mountain Fritillary (*B.napaea*) by the distinct black markings on the under-side of the forewing.

BALKAN FRITILLARY
Boloria graeca
32-34 mm. An inhabitant of high meadows above the tree zone in the Alps and the mountains of the Bal-kans, where it flies in July.

The caterpillar and **chrysalis** are not known.

Identification Rather similar in colour-pattern to the Mountain Fritillary (*B.napaea*) but the margin of the hind wing is more sharply angled and al-most produced into a tail.

BOG FRITILLARY
Proclossiana eunomia
32-36 mm. On the wing in bogs, wet meadows and on moors, up to 1,500 metres, in a single flight between June and August. Found in northern and central Europe (not Britain) and in Arctic Asia and North America.

The caterpillar is mostly grey, marked with white, and has numerous short pink or white spines. It feeds on Bis-tort (*Polygonum bistorta*), Violets (*Viola*) and other plants, and over-winters twice.

The chrysalis is grey, with shiny, silver marks.

Identification The row of black-edged white spots on the underside of the hind wing separates this species from other Fritillaries.

male

Cranberry
Fritillary

Bog
Fritillary

male

male

Balkan
Fritillary

The Small Pearl-bordered Fritillary feeds from various kinds of flower.

SMALL PEARL-BORDERED FRITILLARY
Clossiana selene
36-44 mm. A fairly common butterfly of woodland margins, but occurs also in more open situations, such as meadows and moorland. There is usually a single flight during June and July at high elevations and in the north, but two generations elsewhere, flying in April and May and in July and August. Found throughout Europe (except for Ireland and the extreme south), in temperate Asia across to the Pacific, and in much of North America. Rarely present above 1,500 metres.
The caterpillar is brown, spotted with white, and has short yellow-brown spines. It feeds on Violets (*Viola*), and overwinters in a curled leaf bound with silk.
The chrysalis is purplish-brown and is attached to the foodplant.
Identification Best separated from the similar Pearl-bordered Fritillary (*C.euphrosyne*) by the uniformly coloured, yellow or silver band crossing the end of the cell under the hind wing.

PEARL-BORDERED FRITILLARY
Clossiana euphrosyne
38-46 mm. Locally common in woodland clearings, and attracted to flowers and rotting animal matter. There is a single generation in the north flying during May and June, but two in the south between April and August. Found in most of Europe, including the Arctic and across Asia to the eastern Soviet Union. Occurs up to 1,800 metres in the Alps.
The caterpillar is black, spotted with white, and has numerous yellow and black spines. It feeds on Violets (*Viola*) and overwinters.
The chrysalis is grey, marked with brown, and is suspended from a leaf-stalk or the stem of the foodplant.
Identification The underside of the hind wing is more yellowish, and there are fewer silver spots than on the Small Pearl-bordered Fritillary (*C.selene*).

TITANIA'S FRITILLARY
Clossiana titania
42-46 mm. Flies during July and August in boggy, grassy areas in woods up to 2,000 metres; commonest at about 1,500 metres in coniferous forest. Found in the mountains of southern Europe, southern Finland eastwards to central Asia, and in northern and western North America.
The caterpillar is dark grey, with yellow spines, and feeds on Violets (*Viola*) and Bistort (*Polygonum bistorta*).
The chrysalis is grey-brown, marked with black and white.
Identification Small colour-pattern details of the underside separate this species from other Fritillaries.

**Small
Pearl-bordered
Fritillary**

VIOLET FRITILLARY
Clossiana dia

30-34 mm. Can be common on sunny, grassy slopes and in woodland clearings up to about 1,500 metres. There is a single flight at higher elevations and in the north, but up to three generations in warmer areas between April and October. Found in the mountains of southern Europe, northwards to the Baltic (but not Britain or Scandinavia), and across Asia to western China.

The caterpillar is black or grey, striped with yellow, black and red, and with rows of yellow and white spines. It feeds on Violets (*Viola*), Knotgrasses (*Polygonum*) and other plants. Autumn caterpillars overwinter when partly grown.

The chrysalis is brown, dotted with black.

Identification Similar to the Small Pearl-bordered Fritillary (*C.selene*), but the hind wing is purplish on the underside and is abruptly angled at the outer part of the front edge.

THOR'S FRITILLARY
Clossiana thore

34-38 mm. The single flight of this butterfly appears during late June and July, in grassy, open woodlands in the Alps up to 2,400 metres and in northern Scandinavia. Occurs also in Asia, including Japan.

The caterpillar probably overwinters twice before changing into a chrysalis. It feeds on the leaves of Violets (*Viola*) and Knotgrasses (*Polygonum*).

The chrysalis is not known.

Identification Specimens from the Alps are very dark and distinctive. Scandinavian examples resemble the Small Pearl-bordered Fritillary (*C. selene*), but lack shiny, silver markings on the underside in the basal half of the hind wing.

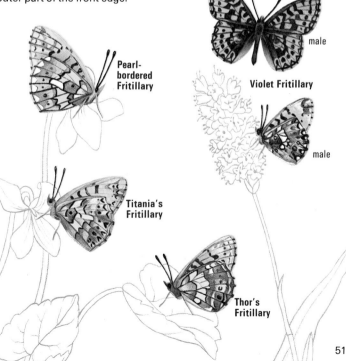

Pearl-bordered Fritillary

Violet Fritillary

male

male

Titania's Fritillary

Thor's Fritillary

male

Freija's Fritillary

Arctic Fritillary

male

FREIJA'S FRITILLARY
Clossiana freija
30-36 mm. A slow-flying, fairly common species of northern Scandinavia and the Baltic countries, and Asia eastwards to Japan; found also in North America. Lives on wet heaths and bogs in Arctic regions with little vegetation. Emerges in May, June or July, depending on the elevation or latitude.

The caterpillar, which overwinters, is blue-grey in colour and is armed with numerous yellowish-green spines. It feeds on Northern Bilberry (*Vaccinium uliginosum*) and Cloudberry (*Rubus chamaemorus*).

The chrysalis is not known.

Identification Probably most like the Arctic Fritillary (*C.chariclea*), but lacks a conspicuous white band across the cell on the underside of the hind wing.

ARCTIC FRITILLARY
Clossiana chariclea
32-34 mm. Probably the most northern of all butterflies and a generally rare species found only in Arctic Europe, northern North America, Greenland, and probably Arctic Asia. On the wing during the short Arctic summer in July and August. Often rests on stones in the sunshine.

The caterpillar and **chrysalis** are not known.

Identification Similar to Frigga's Fritillary (*C.frigga*), but the white markings are less conspicuous on the underside of the hind wing.

POLAR FRITILLARY
Clossiana polaris
30-34 mm. A rare Arctic Scandinavian butterfly found in small, widely separated colonies in dry stony areas. On the wing at the end of June and during July. Found also in Greenland, Arctic Asia, and North America. Flies swiftly, frequently changing direction.

The caterpillar probably feeds on Mountain Avens (*Dryas octopetala*).

The chrysalis is not known.

Identification Easily separated from other Arctic Fritillaries by the numerous white markings on the underside of the hind wing.

FRIGGA'S FRITILLARY
Clossiana frigga
34-40 mm. Common locally at the end of June and during July, in marshy places and wet moors at low elevations and in mountain valleys. Found in countries on the eastern edge of the Baltic northwards to the Arctic, in northern Asia, and in northern and western North America.

The caterpillar, which overwinters, feeds on Cloudberry (*Rubus chamaemorus*). It is brown in colour, striped with lighter brown, and is covered with brown spines.

The chrysalis is not known.

Identification Similar to the Arctic Fritillary (*C.chariclea*), but the white markings on the underside of the hind wing are much more conspicuous.

DUSKY-WINGED FRITILLARY
Clossiana improba
26-28 mm. Emerges in July and can be locally common in dry, open, mountainous areas up to 1,000 metres. There always appear to be more males than females throughout the flight period. Found in Arctic regions of Scandinavia and Russia, and in North America.

The caterpillar is not known, but possibly feeds on Dwarf Willow (*Salix herbacea*).

The chrysalis in unknown.

Identification This is a distinctively small, dull-coloured Fritillary.

male

Dusky-winged Fritillary

male

Polar Fritillary

Frigga's Fritillary

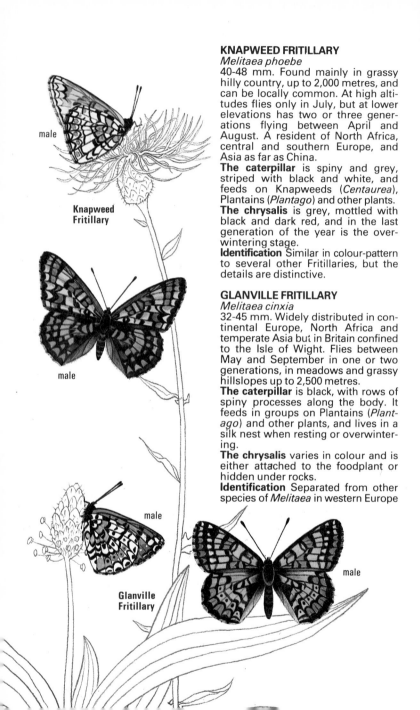

KNAPWEED FRITILLARY
Melitaea phoebe
40-48 mm. Found mainly in grassy hilly country, up to 2,000 metres, and can be locally common. At high altitudes flies only in July, but at lower elevations has two or three generations flying between April and August. A resident of North Africa, central and southern Europe, and Asia as far as China.

The caterpillar is spiny and grey, striped with black and white, and feeds on Knapweeds (*Centaurea*), Plantains (*Plantago*) and other plants.

The chrysalis is grey, mottled with black and dark red, and in the last generation of the year is the overwintering stage.

Identification Similar in colour-pattern to several other Fritillaries, but the details are distinctive.

GLANVILLE FRITILLARY
Melitaea cinxia
32-45 mm. Widely distributed in continental Europe, North Africa and temperate Asia but in Britain confined to the Isle of Wight. Flies between May and September in one or two generations, in meadows and grassy hillslopes up to 2,500 metres.

The caterpillar is black, with rows of spiny processes along the body. It feeds in groups on Plantains (*Plantago*) and other plants, and lives in a silk nest when resting or overwintering.

The chrysalis varies in colour and is either attached to the foodplant or hidden under rocks.

Identification Separated from other species of *Melitaea* in western Europe

Knapweed Fritillary

male

male

male

Glanville Fritillary

male

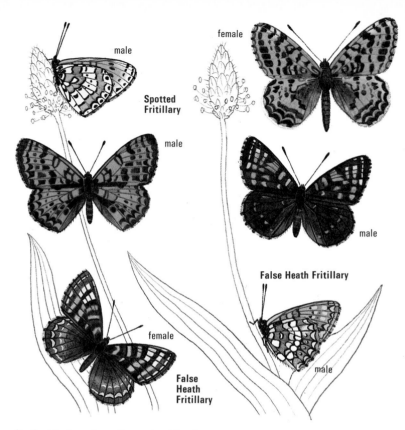

male

female

Spotted Fritillary

male

male

False Heath Fritillary

female

False Heath Fritillary

male

by the black spots on the underside of the hind wing.

SPOTTED FRITILLARY
Melitaea didyma
36-42 mm. Flies in grassy or stony areas in usually two or three generations, and often common up to 1,800 metres. Found in the southern half of Europe, North Africa and central Asia.
The caterpillar feeds on Speedwells (*Veronica*), Plantains (*Plantago*) and several other plants. It is grey, ringed with black, and has rows of light-coloured spines along the body. Caterpillars of the last generation of the year overwinter.
The chrysalis is green, marked with black and orange.
Identification A variable butterfly difficult to separate from other *Melitaea* species.

FALSE HEATH FRITILLARY
Melitaea diamina
36-42 mm. A common alpine species in damp meadows up to 2,000 metres but rare in the lowlands. There is usually one generation, flying between June and August. Found in much of Europe, but not Britain or northern Scandinavia, and in temperate Asia as far as Japan.
The caterpillar is spiny and black-striped, and feeds in groups on Valerian (*Valeriana officinalis*) and several other plants. It hibernates when young, and after the winter feeds singly.
The chrysalis is grey, marked with black and red.
Identification Difficult to distinguish, but the upper side is characteristically rather blackish.

male

**Meadow
Fritillary**

male

female

male

Heath Fritillary

male

HEATH FRITILLARY
Mellicta athalia
36-42 mm. One of the most common Fritillaries in Europe on heaths, in grassland and in woodland clearings up to 1;800 metres. There is a single midsummer flight in the north, but two generations are on the wing in the south between May and September. Found locally in southern England, and widely distributed in continental Europe including the Arctic. Present also in Asia as far east as Japan.

The caterpillar is black, spotted with white, and covered with short, hairy spines. It feeds with others in a web on Plantains (*Plantago*), Cow-wheat (*Melampyrum pratense*) and on other plants. Autumn-generation caterpillars overwinter.

The chrysalis is white, marked with black and orange, and hangs from a stem of the foodplant or neighbouring plants.

Identification Most specimens are separable from other species of *Mellicta* by details of the colour-pattern on the underside of the hind wing. The Provençal Fritillary (*Mellicta deione*, not illustrated) may, however, be impossible to distinguish from the Heath Fritillary without examining internal structures.

MEADOW FRITILLARY
Mellicta parthenoides
30-38 mm. A butterfly of damp hill
and mountain slopes up to 2,000
metres and not usually found below
500 metres. Generally rare, and occur-
ing in widely separated colonies.
Flies in June and July at high elevations, but on the wing elsewhere in
two generations between May and
September. Restricted to western
Europe, but absent from Britain and
Scandinavia.
The caterpillar is black, spotted with
pale blue, and is covered with dull red
spines. It feeds on Plantains (*Plantago*), Speedwells (*Veronica*) and other
plants, and the autumn generation
overwinters.
The chrysalis is grey, marked with
white and black.
Identification Similar to Grison's Fritillary (*M.varia*), but on the upper side
differs in small details of the markings towards the rear edge of the
forewing. Usually flies at lower elevations than Grison's Fritillary.

GRISON'S FRITILLARY
Mellicta varia
28-36 mm. Found only in mountain
pastures of the Alps and Apennines
between 1,800 and 2,500 metres,
where it can be locally common. Appears during June, July and August
in a single flight.
The caterpillar feeds on Plantains
(*Plantago*), Speedwells (*Veronica*),
Cow-wheats (*Melampyrum*) and Gentians (*Gentiana*).
The chrysalis is unknown.
Identification See Meadow Fritillary
(*M.parthenoides*).

NICKERL'S FRITILLARY
Mellicta aurelia
30-32 mm. Common in places in the
mountains up to about 1,500 metres,
flying on moors and in meadows and
bogs, often near woods. Emerges in
June or July, or in two flights between
May and August in some southern
localities. Found only in central and
south-eastern Europe (not Britain),
and eastwards to the central Soviet
Union.
The caterpillar is black, marked with
white and yellow, and is covered in
black spines. It feeds on Plantains
(*Plantago*) and Speedwells (*Veronica*).
Autumn-generation caterpillars overwinter.
The chrysalis is not known.
Identification Similar to the Heath
Fritillary (*M.athalia*), but the lines on
the forewing are more regularly
marked. Assmann's Fritillary (*Mellicta
britomartis*, not illustrated) may be
indistinguishable from Nickerl's Friti-
lary without an examination of internal structures.

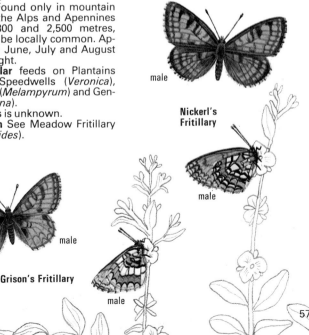

male

**Nickerl's
Fritillary**

male

Grison's Fritillary

male

male

male

Scarce Fritillary

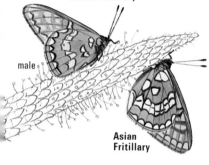

male

Asian Fritillary

SCARCE FRITILLARY
Hypodryas maturna
40-48 mm. A strongly flying species of grassy places, usually at low elevations and often near water. Found in a few widely scattered colonies in Europe north of the Alps and in western Asia, but absent from Britain and northern Scandinavia. There is a single emergence during May and June.

The caterpillar spins a web and at first feeds in a group on Ash (*Fraxinus*) or other trees. In the autumn the leaves and webs drop to the ground, where the caterpillar remains all winter. In the spring it changes diet and feeds singly on Plantains (*Plantago*) and other small plants. The full-grown caterpillar is yellow, striped with black, and covered with black spines.

The chrysalis is pale green or yellow, marked with black and yellow, and is formed under a stone or on a tree trunk.

Identification Not likely to be confused with other Fritillaries in western Europe.

ASIAN FRITILLARY
Hypodryas intermedia
34-42 mm. Commonest at about 1,500 metres in grassy, flowery places in woods. Flies at the end of June and during July in a single generation. Found in the Alps and through temperate Asia to Korea.

The caterpillar feeds on Cow-wheats (*Melampyrum*), Plantains (*Plantago*) and Speedwells (*Veronica*), and overwinters from September to spring.

The chrysalis is not known.

Identification Males are fairly distinctive. Females are similar to the female Cynthia's Fritillary (*H.cynthia*), differing only on the underside of the hind wing, where the yellow band across the end of the cell encloses a thin black line.

LAPLAND FRITILLARY
Hypodryas iduna
36-40 mm. Found in small, widely separated colonies in Arctic Scandinavia and in some western and central Asian mountains. Usually occurs at about 600 metres on moors or in marshy areas in woods. On the wing at the end of June and during July in a single generation.

The caterpillar and **chrysalis** are not known.

Identification A distinctively banded butterfly on both wing surfaces.

CYNTHIA'S FRITILLARY
Hypodryas cynthia
36-42 mm. A butterfly of the Alps and the mountains of Bulgaria, on moors, heaths and in meadows up to about 3,000 metres. Common above the tree zone in some areas in a single flight during July and August.

The caterpillar is black, marked with yellow, and has rows of black spines along the body. It feeds in a group on Plantains (*Plantago*), Louseworts (*Pedicularis*) and other plants, and overwinters in a web.

The chrysalis is greyish-white, marked with black and yellow.

Identification Males are fairly distinctive. The female is much like that of the Asian Fritillary (*H.intermedia*), but has a uniformly yellow band crossing the end of the cell under the hind wing.

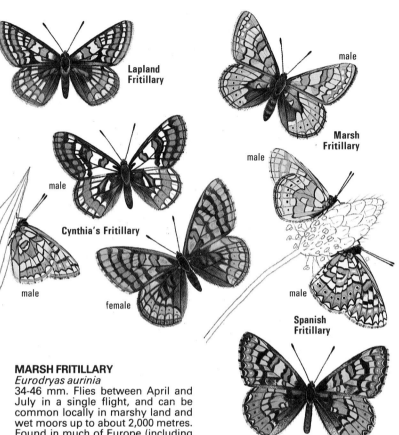

Lapland
Fritillary

male

Marsh
Fritillary

male

male

Cynthia's Fritillary

male

male

female

Spanish
Fritillary

female

MARSH FRITILLARY
Eurodryas aurinia
34-46 mm. Flies between April and
July in a single flight, and can be
common locally in marshy land and
wet moors up to about 2,000 metres.
Found in much of Europe (including
Britain, but excluding northern Scandinavia), in North Africa and in temperate Asia eastwards to Korea.
The caterpillar, which overwinters,
spins a web and lives in a large group
on Plantains (*Plantago*), Gentians
(*Gentiana*) and other plants. It is
mostly black, marked with white, and
has several short, black spines along
the body.
The chrysalis is white, with black and
orange markings. It is suspended
from the foodplant or nearby vegetation.
Identification Separable from other
similarly patterned Fritillaries by the
combination of a strongly marked
upper side and a usually pale underside to the forewing.

SPANISH FRITILLARY
Eurodryas desfontainii
34-40 mm. Occurs only in the mountains of North Africa, Spain and
Portugal and in the French Pyrenees,
up to about 1,500 metres and usually
on south-facing slopes.
The caterpillar feeds on Knapweeds
(*Centaurea*), Scabious (*Knautia*) and
other plants, and probably overwinters.
The chrysalis is not known.
Identification Resembles the Marsh
Fritillary (*E.aurinia*), but has conspicuous black markings on the underside
of the forewing.

male

Marbled White

BROWNS
Family Satyridae

A large family of about 3,000 species, and commonest in temperate regions with over 100 species in Europe. Most have eye-spots on the wings but some tropical American species have almost completely transparent wings. The caterpillars are usually green or brown, finely hairy, tapered at both ends and have a short, forked tail. They feed on Grasses, Palms and related plants. The chrysalids either hang from tail hooks or are formed on the ground.

female

MARBLED WHITE
Melanargia galathea
45-56 mm. A common butterfly of open, flowery grassland up to 1,800 metres. Flies in June and July in a single generation and has a characteristic, slow flight. Found in southern and central Europe, including southern England, and in North Africa and the Middle East.
The caterpillar is green or brown; it hibernates soon after hatching, and starts to feed early the next year on Fescues (*Festuca*) and other Grasses.
The chrysalis is mainly brown and yellow, and is hidden at the base of the Grasses.
Identification Similar to Esper's Marbled White (*M.russiae*), but lacks a dark line across the cell at the base of the forewing.

**Esper's
Marbled White**

**Western
Marbled White**

In spite of its name, the Western Marbled White is a Brown butterfly (Family Satyridae). Its resting position is typical of sun-basking species.

ESPER'S MARBLED WHITE
Melanargia russiae
42-56 mm. Rather rare and local in most of Europe, and prefers rocky slopes with little vegetation up to about 1,800 metres in elevation. Found in Spain and Portugal, southern France, Italy and across temperate Asia to Siberia. On the wing usually in June and July for about two weeks.
The caterpillar, which overwinters, feeds on Annual Meadow Grass (*Poa annua*), *Lamarckia aurea* and on other Grasses. It is green, striped with dark green on the back, and with yellow and white on the sides.
The chrysalis is yellowish-brown.
Identification Differs from the similarly coloured Marbled White (*M. galathea*) in the presence of a dark band across the cell at the base of the forewing.

WESTERN MARBLED WHITE
Melanargia occitanica
50-56 mm. A locally common butterfly of rocky mountain slopes up to 1,800 metres, where it flies between April and June in a single generation. Found in south-western and central southern Europe and in North Africa.
The caterpillar feeds on False Brome (*Brachypodium*) and other Grasses. It is brownish-grey, striped on the sides with yellow, and has a green head. The caterpillar is the overwintering stage.
The chrysalis is light brown, marked with dark brown.
Identification Similar to Esper's Marbled White (*M.russiae*) in colour-pattern, but the line crossing the cell on the forewing is less irregular in shape, and the veins on the underside of the hind wing are brown.

female

Woodland
Grayling

male

male

R

WOODLAND GRAYLING
Hipparchia fagi
65-76 mm. A locally common butter-fly of open woodlands and scrubland, usually below 1,000 metres. Often rests on tree-trunks, where it is well camouflaged. Usually emerges in July and August in a single flight. Found in temperate western Asia and in central and southern Europe, ex-cept for Britain, north-western con-tinental Europe and Scandinavia.
The caterpillar is brown, striped with dark brown and yellow, and feeds at night on Creeping Soft Grass (*Holcus*

mollis) and other Grasses. It over-winters.
The chrysalis is brown, and is formed on the ground at the base of the Grass.
Identification Not difficult to separate from other European Graylings, ex-cept for the Rock Grayling (*Hipparchia alcyone*, not illustrated), which is very similar to the Woodland Gray-ling in colour-pattern but is almost always smaller in size.

CORSICAN GRAYLING
Hipparchia neomiris
38-44 mm. Confined to the mountains of Sardinia, Corsica and Elba, where the single yearly generation flies in June and July. Sometimes common on Pine-forested slopes.

The caterpillar and **chrysalis** are not known.

Identification Separable from all other western European Graylings by the colour-pattern of the upper side of the wings.

Corsican Grayling

GRAYLING
Hipparchia semele
48-60 mm. Widespread and common in open, grassy places and on heaths up to 1,500 metres in a single flight between May and September. Often visits Thyme (*Thymus*) flowers, but usually rests on the ground with the closed wings inclined towards the sun so that little shadow is cast, making the butterfly difficult to detect. Found in most of Europe, except for southern Italy and northern Scandinavia, and in western Asia.

The caterpillar is yellow, striped along the body with brown and dull yellow. It feeds on various kinds of Grass and overwinters when half grown.

The chrysalis is brown, and formed inside a loosely woven cocoon on or near the surface of the ground.

Identification May be confused with the Southern Grayling (*Hipparchia aristaeus*, not illustrated), which may fly with the Grayling in parts of south-eastern Europe and is probably in-distinguishable from it except by an examination of internal structures.

male

Grayling

female

male

TREE GRAYLING

Neohipparchia statilinus

46-53 mm. Locally common, but becoming more rare in some areas. On the wing between July and October, in a single flight, the males always emerging several days before the females. Found on heaths and in rocky places on mountain slopes in southern and central Europe (not Britain or Scandinavia) and in western Asia.

The caterpillar is yellow, striped with brown, and feeds on Fescues (*Festuca*), Meadow Grass (*Poa*) and other Grasses. It overwinters, partly grown, at the base of the Grass.

The chrysalis is not known.

Identification Distinctively marked and not likely to be mistaken for any other western European Grayling.

STRIPED GRAYLING

Pseudotergumia fidia

48-52 mm. Prefers dry, stony slopes with a few trees, up to 1,500 metres. Flies in July and August in one generation and can be common locally in North Africa, Spain and Portugal, southern France and the western Alps of Italy.

The caterpillar is yellow or brown, striped along the body with black or yellow. It feeds on grasses and probably overwinters.

The chrysalis is pale brown, with darker brown wings.

Identification Probably most like the Tree Grayling (*Neohipparchia statilinus*) in colour-pattern, but is distinctively marked on the underside of the wings.

Tree Grayling female

male

male

male

Striped Grayling

male

THE HERMIT
Chazara briseis
40-52 mm. The single yearly generation flies between May and September, chiefly in dry, grassy places in chalk or limestone regions, up to 1,800 metres in the mountains of Spain. Found in central and southern Europe, North Africa and western Asia, but not in Britain, north-western France, northern Germany or Scandinavia.

The caterpillar is greyish-yellow, striped with grey. It feeds on Fescues (*Festuca*) and other Grasses, and overwinters at the base of the food-plant.

The chrysalis is a shiny brown and is formed amongst the Grass roots just below the surface of the soil.

Identification A very variable species, but likely to be confused only with the Southern Hermit (*Chazara prieuri*, not illustrated), a solely North African and Spanish butterfly that has a much more clearly marked pattern on the underside of the hind wing.

male

The Hermit

male

ALPINE GRAYLING
Oeneis glacialis
48-52 mm. Commonest near the upper edge of the tree zone in grassy, rocky areas, but only in isolated colonies. Appears in a single flight, usually in July, and is attracted to flowers. Found only in the Alps.
The caterpillar is reddish-grey, striped with brown, and feeds on Sheep's Fescue (*Festuca ovina*). It overwinters twice before changing into a chrysalis.
The chrysalis is hidden amongst the Grass roots.
Identification Similar to the Norse Grayling (*O.norna*), but the veins on the underside of the hind wing are outlined with greyish-white.

NORSE GRAYLING
Oeneis norna
40-44 mm. Flies in July on moors, bogs, or wet grassland and is locally common. Found only in Arctic Scandinavia and Finland and in some central Asian mountain ranges.
The caterpillar feeds on Grasses and perhaps Sedges (*Carex*), but has not been described.
The chrysalis is not known.
Identification Probably closest to the Alpine Grayling (*O.glacialis*), but has dark brown veins on the underside of the hind wing.

Norse Grayling

male

Alpine
Grayling

male

ARCTIC GRAYLING
Oeneis bore
40-43 mm. A rare butterfly of dry, stony slopes in Arctic Scandinavia, Finland, the northern Soviet Union, and North America. Usually found at low elevations in the north, but up to 600 metres in the south of its range. Appears in a single flight during June and July.

The caterpillar, which overwinters twice, is dull yellow, striped with brown, and feeds on Sheep's Fescue (*Festuca ovina*).

The chrysalis is green and yellow, marked with dark and light green and black.

Identification Lacks eye-spots on the wings, unlike other Arctic species of Grayling.

BALTIC GRAYLING
Oeneis jutta
43-50 mm. Prefers boggy places near coniferous forests at low elevations. Emerges during June and July in a single flight. Males in particular often rest on tree-trunks. Found throughout the Arctic and the northern part of the Northern Hemisphere from Scandinavia across northern Asia to Alaska and northern Canada. Flies every year, but the caterpillar overwinters twice, and odd-year butterflies are slightly different in colour-pattern from even-year butterflies.

The caterpillar is brown, striped with darker brown, and feeds on Grasses.

The chrysalis is not known.

Identification Distinguished by the small, yellow eye-spots on the upper side.

male

Arctic Grayling

male

Baltic Grayling

male

male

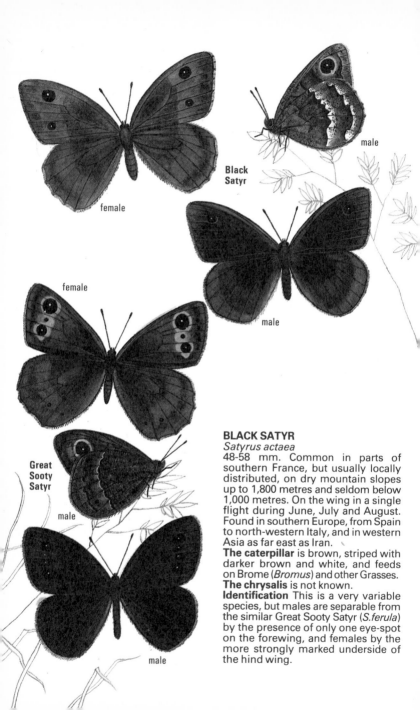

Black Satyr

female

male

female

male

Great Sooty Satyr

male

male

BLACK SATYR
Satyrus actaea
48-58 mm. Common in parts of southern France, but usually locally distributed, on dry mountain slopes up to 1,800 metres and seldom below 1,000 metres. On the wing in a single flight during June, July and August. Found in southern Europe, from Spain to north-western Italy, and in western Asia as far east as Iran.

The caterpillar is brown, striped with darker brown and white, and feeds on Brome (*Bromus*) and other Grasses.

The chrysalis is not known.

Identification This is a very variable species, but males are separable from the similar Great Sooty Satyr (*S.ferula*) by the presence of only one eye-spot on the forewing, and females by the more strongly marked underside of the hind wing.

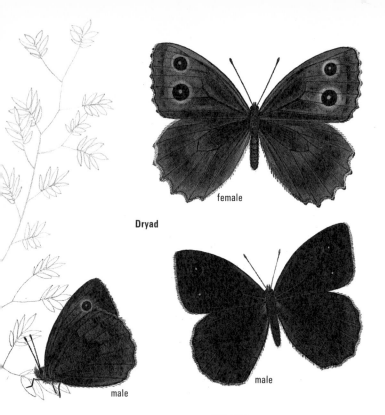

female

Dryad

male

male

GREAT SOOTY SATYR
Satyrus ferula
46-50 mm. Emerges in a single flight between June and August on rocky slopes from 500-1,500 metres in the Alps and the mountains of Italy and the Balkans, but absent from Spain and Portugal. Also flies in North Africa above 1,500 metres in the Atlas mountains and in south-western Asia as far east as the Himalayas.
The caterpillar is brown, with dark brown and white stripes. It feeds on Grasses and overwinters.
The chrysalis is not known.
Identification Most like the Dryad (*Minois dryas*), but has white centres to the eye-spots on the upper side of the forewing.

DRYAD
Minois dryas
54-63 mm. A butterfly of damp moors and meadows, often near woods, usually below 1,000 metres. Usually emerges in July and August in a single generation, flying quite slowly and close to the ground. Occurs in colonies in central Europe (not Britain or Scandinavia), and in temperate Asia, including Japan.
The caterpillar is yellow-grey, striped with dark grey and brown. It feeds on Purple Moor Grass (*Molinia caerulea*) and other Grasses, and overwinters partly grown.
The chrysalis is brown and grey, and is formed on the surface of the ground.
Identification Separable from the Great Sooty Satyr (*Satyrus ferula*) by the blue-centred eye-spots on the forewing.

GREAT BANDED GRAYLING
Brintesia circe
65-73 mm. Common at times in open Oak woods at low elevations during June, July and August in a single flight. Often rests on tree-trunks or branches, and if disturbed flies long distances before resettling. Resident in southern and central Europe (as far north as central France and Germany) and in south-western Asia.

The caterpillar is brown, striped with black and darker brown, and feeds on Rye-grass (*Lolium*) and other Grasses. It overwinters partly grown.

The chrysalis is brown, spotted with yellow.

Identification The white-banded wings of this species are distinctive.

FALSE GRAYLING
Arethusana arethusa
43-48 mm. Locally distributed in grassy, rocky places up to 1,000 metres, usually in limestone or chalk regions. Flies in a single generation during July and August, often resting on the ground. Found in North Africa, southern and central Europe (not Britain, the Low Countries or Scandinavia) and in temperate western and central Asia.

The caterpillar is grey, striped with dark grey, orange and yellow, and feeds on Grasses. It overwinters.

The chrysalis is brown, and is formed amongst the Grass roots.

Identification A very variable butterfly, but the upper-side colour-pattern is usually distinctive.

male

male

Great Banded Grayling

False Grayling

male

male

male

Arran
Brown

Large
Ringlet

female

male

Lapland
Ringlet

ARRAN BROWN
Erebia ligea
48-55 mm. On the wing in a single flight during June, July and August, and locally common in hilly, grassy places in or near woods up to 1,500 metres. Usually rests on Grasses and sometimes visits flowers. Found in parts of Scandinavia, France, the mountains of southern Europe and in temperate Asia as far east as Japan. Records from Arran, which gave this butterfly its name, Scotland, are doubtful.
The caterpillar is greyish-yellow, striped with brown and white, and feeds on Millet (*Milium*) and other Grasses. It overwinters either inside the unbroken egg-shell or as a newly hatched caterpillar, and may overwinter a second time.
The chrysalis is brown, marked with black, and lies on the surface of the ground.
Identification Very variable in colour-pattern but usually separable from the Large Ringlet (*E.euryale*) by the more strongly marked underside of the hind wing.

LARGE RINGLET
Erebia euryale
44-46 mm. Sometimes very common in grassy places from 1,000 metres to the upper edge of the tree zone in mountainous country. On the wing during July in a single flight, often visiting Ragwort (*Senecio*) flowers. Present in northern Spain, the Pyrenees and Alps, and areas eastwards to the mountains of western and central Asia.
The caterpillar is yellow-brown, striped with white, black and yellow. It feeds on Grasses and overwinters twice.
The chrysalis is dull yellow.
Identification See Arran Brown (*E. ligea*).

LAPLAND RINGLET
Erebia embla
40-45 mm. In Europe, found only in northern Scandinavia and Finland in bogs and on wet moors in a single flight between the end of May and July. Elsewhere, a resident in northern Asia eastwards to the Pacific coast.
The caterpillar and **chrysalis** are not known.
Identification Distinguished from other species of *Erebia* by the absence of white centres to the black spots on the upper side of the hind wing.

71

ARCTIC RINGLET
Erebia disa
44-47 mm. Lives in marshy grassland and moors, including areas that are regularly flooded, usually at low elevations. The single flight is in June and early July. Found in Arctic Scandinavia and Finland and across northern Asia, Alaska and Canada.
The caterpillar and **chrysalis** are not known.
Identification Fairly easy to identify because of the lack of spots on both sides of the wings.

ARCTIC WOODLAND RINGLET
Erebia polaris
35-38 mm. Found only in Arctic Europe and Asia, where there is a single flight at the end of June and during July in meadows below 300 metres.
The caterpillar and **chrysalis** are not known.
Identification Similar in colour-pattern to the Woodland Ringlet (*Erebia medusa*, not illustrated), but the latter is a central and southern European species and does not occur in the Arctic.

ERIPHYLE RINGLET
Erebia eriphyle
28-30 mm. A rare and local species, on the wing during July in a single flight. Found in grassy places, often on north-facing slopes between 1,200 and 2,000 metres, and only in the Alps.
The caterpillar feeds on Grasses and overwinters.
The chrysalis is not known.
Identification Similar to high-elevation specimens of the Yellow-spotted Ringlet (*E.manto*), but the red spots on the underside of the hind wing are slightly smaller.

YELLOW-SPOTTED RINGLET
Erebia manto
28-32 mm. Locally common near or above the upper edge of the tree zone in meadows and grassy slopes in the mountains of southern Europe from the Pyrenees to the Balkans. The single flight takes place between June and August.
The caterpillar, which overwinters, is yellow-brown, marked with black, and

feeds on Grasses.
The chrysalis is yellow, marked with black, and is formed on the ground.
Identification See the Eriphyle Ringlet (*E.eriphyle*).

BLIND RINGLET
Erebia pharte
29-32 mm. A butterfly of damp meadows in the Alps and the Tatra mountains of Poland and Czechoslovakia; usually found above 1,500 metres near the upper limit of the tree zone. Emerges between July and September in a single flight.
The caterpillar feeds on Grasses and overwinters.
The chrysalis is not known.
Identification Resembles the widespread Mountain Ringlet (*E.epiphron*), but lacks black spots on the forewing.

LESSER MOUNTAIN RINGLET
Erebia melampus
29-32 mm. Widely distributed and common between 1,400 and 2,400 metres in grassy places. On the wing in a single flight during June, July and August, and found only in the Alps.
The caterpillar, which overwinters, is green, with pink and dark-green stripes along the body. It feeds on Meadow Grass (*Poa*) and other Grasses.
The chrysalis is grey and formed on the ground.
Identification Usually lacks a black spot within the apical red spot on the forewing, but is otherwise similar to the Sudeten Ringlet (*Erebia sudetica*, not illustrated), which is usually not found above 1,200 metres in the Alps.

MOUNTAIN RINGLET
Erebia epiphron
35-40 mm. Appears during June and July in a single flight in northern Britain (not Ireland), but is more widespread in the mountains of southern Europe from the Pyrenees to the Carpathians. Flies in wet, grassy forest clearings and on moors up to 3,000 metres, usually close to the ground.
The caterpillar is green, striped with yellow and white, and feeds on Hairgrass (*Deschampsia*) and other

Arctic Ringlet

male

Yellow-spotted Ringlet

male

male

Arctic Woodland Ringlet

male

female

Eriphyle Ringlet

Blind Ringlet

Lesser Mountain Ringlet

Grasses. It overwinters partly grown.
The chrysalis is either pale green or greenish-white, and lies on the ground in a loosely woven cocoon of Grass and silk.
Identification Possibly most like the Lesser Mountain Ringlet (*E.melampus*), but the black spots under the hind wing have narrow red margins. The Pyrenean Descimon's Ringlet (*Erebia serotina*, not illustrated), known from only a few specimens, is also like the Mountain Ringlet.

Mountain Ringlet

Scotch Argus
male

male

Sooty Ringlet

Almond-eyed Ringlet

SCOTCH ARGUS
Erebia aethiops
40-53 mm. The single flight of this species takes place between July and early September, the butterflies seldom taking to the wing unless the weather is sunny. Found in Scotland and northern England, central and south-eastern Europe and in western Asia. Restricted to grassy areas, usually near forests in hills and mountains up to 2,000 metres, but also occurs near the coast in Belgium.
The caterpillar is usually yellow-brown, striped with darker and lighter brown. It feeds on Couch Grass (*Agropyron*) and other Grasses, and overwinters when partly grown.
The chrysalis is dull yellow, striped with brown, and lies amongst the Grass roots in a frail cocoon of silk and Grass.
Identification Separable from other species of *Erebia* by the white-dotted, pale band under the hind wing. De Prunner's Ringlet (*Erebia triaria*, not illustrated) is similar to the Scotch Argus, but the pale band under the hind wing is poorly defined.

ALMOND-EYED RINGLET
Erebia alberganus
38-43 mm. Forms isolated colonies in mountain meadows, usually in or near woods, from about 1,000 to 2,000 metres. Emerges in a single flight between late June and August in the Alps, the mountains of Italy and in Bulgaria.
The caterpillar is green, striped with white and brown, and feeds on Fescues (*Festuca*) and other Grasses. It probably overwinters.
The chrysalis is light yellow and brown.
Identification Resembles the Bright-eyed Ringlet (*E.oeme*, page 78), but the orange markings on the upper side of the wings are ovate or pointed, not round.

SOOTY RINGLET
Erebia pluto
35-44 mm. A solely alpine, locally common butterfly ranging from southern France to Austria. The single generation flies mainly during July and August in rock-strewn grassy places, generally above 1,800 metres on mountain slopes.
The caterpillar is green, striped with dark green, and feeds on Grasses. It overwinters partly grown.
The chrysalis is not known.
Identification Varies in colour-pattern, but is generally distinctive amongst other alpine species of *Erebia*.

male
Silky Ringlet

Spring Ringlet
male

male

False Mnestra Ringlet

male

Gavarnie Ringlet

SILKY RINGLET
Erebia gorge
30-37 mm. Often common at high elevations up to 3,000 metres in fields near rocky slopes. Emerges during June and July in a single flight in the mountains of southern Europe from the Pyrenees to the Balkans.
The caterpillar is not known, but probably feeds on Grasses.
The chrysalis is brown and green.
Identification The eye-spots of this species may be either present or absent, but the rather shiny, silky surface of the upper side of the wings is distinctive.

FALSE MNESTRA RINGLET
Erebia aethiopella
30-34 mm. Found on grassy mountain slopes above 1,800 metres in the Alps and mountains of the Balkans. Can be common locally during the single flight in July and August.
The caterpillar and **chrysalis** are not known.
Identification Some specimens lack eye-spots and can be confused with the alpine Mnestra's Ringlet (*Erebia mnestra*, not illustrated), but in *Erebia aethiopella* the red band on the upper side of the hind wing extends beyond the middle of the wing.

GAVARNIE RINGLET
Erebia gorgone
33-38 mm. Locally common in a single flight during July and August on rocky mountain sides above 1,500 metres. Found only in the Pyrenees.
The caterpillar feeds on Alpine Meadow Grass (*Poa alpina*) and other Grasses.
The chrysalis is not known.
Identification Separable from Pyrenean specimens of the Silky Ringlet (*E.gorge*) by the less shiny upper side, and by the presence of three eye-spots on the upper side of the forewing in most specimens.

SPRING RINGLET
Erebia epistygne
40-45 mm. Occurs in colonies, usually between 500 and 2,000 metres, on stony fields in open country or in woodlands. The single generation flies early in spring, the timing dependent on the altitude. Found only in Spain and south-eastern France.
The caterpillar feeds on Creeping Fescue (*Festuca rubra*) and other Grasses.
The chrysalis is not known.
Identification The yellow band on the forewing separates this butterfly from all other European Ringlets.

SWISS BRASSY RINGLET
Erebia tyndarus
29-31 mm. A butterfly of fields and meadows between 1,800 and 2,500 metres in the Alps, from near Mont Blanc to western Austria. Usually on the wing during July and August in a single flight.

The caterpillar can be grey, yellow or green, striped with darker or paler lines. It feeds on Grasses and probably overwinters.

The chrysalis is not known.

Identification Separable from the Common Brassy Ringlet (*E.cassioides*) by the less sharply pointed forewing.

COMMON BRASSY RINGLET
Erebia cassioides
30-33 mm. The single flight of this generally common species is between June and September on grassy slopes from 1,500 to 1,800 metres. Found in the mountains of southern Europe from the Pyrenees to the Balkans.

The caterpillar is similar to that of the Swiss Brassy Ringlet but has broader stripes along the side. It feeds on Grasses and overwinters.

The chrysalis is not known.

Identification Probably most like the Swiss Brassy Ringlet (*E.tyndarus*), but has more strongly pointed forewings. Similar also to the Ottoman Brassy Ringlet (*Erebia ottomana*, not illustrated), but the latter flies a few weeks later and is smaller.

SPANISH BRASSY RINGLET
Erebia hispania
30-36 mm. Common in colonies on dry, grassy slopes between 1,500 and 2,500 metres in the Pyrenees and mountains of southern Spain. There is a single flight during June and July.

The caterpillar feeds on Annual Meadow Grass (*Poa annua*) and other Grasses.

The chrysalis is not known.

Identification Fairly similar to the Common Brassy Ringlet (*E.cassioides*), but has a distinctively marked forewing.

WATER RINGLET
Erebia pronoe
42-48 mm. Flies in woodland clearings and on damp, grassy slopes, and is locally common between 1,000 and 2,000 metres. Emerges in a single flight during July, August and September in the mountains of southern Europe from the Pyrenees to the Balkans.

The caterpillar is a dull orange, striped along the body with black and brown. It feeds on Meadow Grasses (*Poa*) and other Grasses, and overwinters.

The chrysalis is pale yellow and brown.

Common Brassy Ringlet

male

male

Swiss Brassy Ringlet

male

Spanish Brassy Ringlet

male

Lefèbvre's Ringlet

Larche Ringlet

male

female

Water Ringlet

Autumn Ringlet

Identification Similar on the upper side of the wings to the Scotch Argus (*E.aethiops*, page 74), but differs in the colour-pattern of the underside of the hind wing. The Stygian Ringlet (*Erebia styx*, not illustrated), from the central and eastern Alps, differs in the brownish-grey underside of the hind wing. The Marbled Ringlet (*Erebia montana*, not illustrated), from the Alps and Apennines, resembles *E. styx*, but the veins on the underside of the hind wing are white.

LEFÈBVRE'S RINGLET
Erebia lefebvrei
34-40 mm. Widespread and sometimes common in rocky parts of the Pyrenees and mountains of northern Spain, seldom below 1,500 metres. Usually appears during July or August in a single flight.
The caterpillar feeds on Sheep's Fescue (*Festuca ovina*) and other Grasses. It probably overwinters.
The chrysalis is not known.
Identification The male is fairly distinctive. The female resembles the Piedmont Ringlet (*E.meolans*, page 78), another Pyrenean butterfly, but lacks a conspicuous pale band on the underside of the hind wing.

LARCHE RINGLET
Erebia scipio
39-42 mm. Confined to steep rocky places in the Alps of France and northern Italy between 1,500 and 2,500 metres. Probably becoming less common. Emerges during June, July and August in a single flight.
The caterpillar and **chrysalis** are unknown.
Identification The details of the colour-pattern distinguish this species from other alpine Ringlets.

AUTUMN RINGLET
Erebia neoridas
38-48 mm. Forms small, widely separated colonies on uncultivated ground between 500 and 1,500 metres in the Pyrenees, Alps and Apennines. The single yearly flight takes place in August and September.
The caterpillar is yellowish-green, spotted with black, and striped along the body with white.
The chrysalis is not known.
Identification Somewhat similar to the Scotch Argus (*E.aethiops*, page 74), but lacks white spots under the hind wing.

Bright-eyed Ringlet

Dewy Ringlet

male

male

Piedmont Ringlet

male

male

BRIGHT-EYED RINGLET
Erebia oeme
38-44 mm. Fairly common in wet meadows and grassy clearings in woods between 1,200 and 1,600 metres, emerging in a single flight during June and July. Found only in the mountains of southern Europe, but not in the Apennines.

The caterpillar, which overwinters, is a dull yellow, striped with brown. It feeds on Wood-rush (*Luzula*) and Fescue Grasses (*Festuca*).

The chrysalis is yellow, marked with brown.

Identification Several other species of *Erebia* have a similar colour-pattern, but the white centres to the eye-spots on the hind wing are especially conspicuous in this species.

PIEDMONT RINGLET
Erebia meolans
35-43 mm. Widespread and common on rocky slopes between 1,500 and 1,800 metres in the mountains of northern and southern Spain and in the Alps. On the wing in a single flight during July and August.

The caterpillar is green, striped with darker and lighter green. It feeds on Hair-grass (*Deschampsia*) and other Grasses, and overwinters.

The chrysalis is green, marked with black and brown.

Identification Resembles Lefèbvre's Ringlet (*E.lefebvrei*, page 77), but is distinguished by the conspicuous pale band on the underside of the hind wing.

DEWY RINGLET
Erebia pandrose
36-46 mm. A butterfly of stony fields and mountain slopes, and locally common in some years. Emerges in a single flight between the end of June and the beginning of August in Scandinavia and Finland at moderate altitudes, and between 1,500 and 3,000 metres in the mountains of southern Europe. Occurs also in western and central Asia.

The caterpillar is green, striped with black. It feeds on Grasses, and overwinters.

The chrysalis is brown and green, and is formed on the surface of the ground.

Identification Distinctively marked with black spots on the upper side of the wings.

male

Ringlet

male

MEADOW BROWN
Maniola jurtina
44-50 mm. Often very common on Grass and heathland up to about 1,500 metres in much of Europe, including Britain but excluding northern Scandinavia. Found also in Asia as far east as the Ural mountains of central Russia and in North Africa and the Canaries. There is probably only one generation each year, which is on the wing from June to September.
The caterpillar is green, spotted with black, and striped with white and dark green. It feeds on Grasses, often Meadow Grasses (*Poa*), and overwinters partly grown.
The chrysalis is green, marked with yellow, brown and black, and is attached to a Grass stem.
Identification Resembles the Dusky Meadow Brown (*Hyponephele lycaon*, page 80), but has only one eye-spot on the upper side of the forewing.

female

Meadow Brown

RINGLET
Aphantopus hyperantus
40-50 mm. Generally common near and in woods and along old hedgerows up to about 1,500 metres in a single flight during June and July. Often visits flowers. Found in most of Britain and continental Europe (except for southern Spain and Italy and Arctic Scandinavia), and also in northern Asia as far east as Siberia.
The caterpillar, which overwinters, is yellow-brown with darker stripes, and feeds on Meadow Grasses (*Poa*) and other Grasses, and rarely on Sedges (*Carex*).
The chrysalis is yellow-brown and reddish-brown, and lies on the surface of the ground inside a frail cocoon of silk and grass.
Identification Similar to the False Ringlet (*Coenonympha oedippus*, page 84), on the upper side, but the pattern of the spots on the underside is distinctive.

male

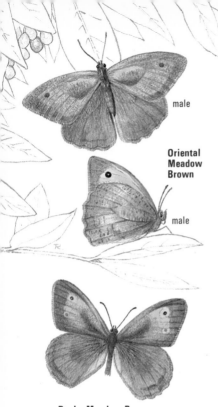

male

Oriental
Meadow
Brown

female

male

Dusky Meadow Brown

ORIENTAL MEADOW BROWN
Hyponephele lupina
38-44 mm. Local in distribution and usually restricted to dry, stony places up to about 2,000 metres in limestone regions. Emerges in a single flight during July and August, often sheltering in bushes. Occurs in North Africa, southern Europe and in temperate Asia as far east as Iran.
The caterpillar feeds on Grasses, and probably overwinters.
The chrysalis is not known.
Identification Very similar to the Dusky Meadow Brown (*H.lycaon*) in colour-pattern, but has a more strongly toothed margin to the hind wing and is usually larger.

GATEKEEPER
Pyronia tithonus
36-42 mm. Common in places, especially near woods and along hedgerows, and often attracted to the flowers of Wood Sage (*Teucrium scorodonia*). Appears in July and August in a single flight, usually at low elevations but up to 1,000 metres in southern Europe. Found in most of Europe but not in Scandinavia or northern Britain.
The caterpillar is either green or brown, striped along the body with black, brown and white. It feeds on Cocksfoot (*Dactylis glomerata*) and other Grasses, and overwinters partly grown.
The chrysalis is brown or green, marked with dark brown and black, and is attached to a Grass stem.
Identification Separable from the Southern Gatekeeper (*P.cecilia*) by the presence of eye-spots on the underside of the hind wing.

DUSKY MEADOW BROWN
Hyponephele lycaon
39-43 mm. Flies during June, July and August, often visiting flowers in forest clearings and other dry, uncultivated areas, usually at low elevations. There is one generation each year. Fairly common in parts of Europe, but not found in Britain, France, the Low Countries or Scandinavia. Occurs also in North Africa and in western and central Asia.
The caterpillar is green, striped with dark green, white and yellow. It feeds on Meadow Grass (*Poa*) and other Grasses, and overwinters.
The chrysalis is brownish-red or green, marked with white or yellow.
Identification Separable from the Meadow Brown (*Maniola jurtina*, page 79) by the presence of two eye-spots on the forewing.

male

Gatekeeper

male

Southern Gatekeeper

male

female

male

SOUTHERN GATEKEEPER
Pyronia cecilia
30-34 mm. Found usually in dry, scrubby places between sea-level and 1,500 metres, in North Africa, Europe south of the Alps and Pyrenees, and in Turkey. Flies between May and August, probably in two or more generations; often common.
The caterpillar is greyish- or pinkish-white, striped with black and grey. It feeds on Tufted Hair-grass (*Deschampsia cespitosa*) and other Grasses. Autumn caterpillars overwinter.
The chrysalis is brown and grey, with black spots.
Identification Lacks eye-spots under the hind wing, unlike the Gatekeeper (*P.tithonus*).

SPANISH GATEKEEPER
Pyronia bathseba
28-38 mm. On the wing between April and July, probably in more than one generation, along hedgerows and in uncultivated country. Found up to 800 metres in Spain and as high as 1,800 metres in North Africa, and occurs also in Portugal and southern France.
The caterpillar is yellowish-grey, striped with grey. It feeds on Grasses, and probably overwinters.
The chrysalis is brown.
Identification The distinctive colour-pattern separates this butterfly from all other European Browns.

male

male

Spanish Gatekeeper

female

LARGE HEATH
Coenonympha tullia
35-40 mm. A butterfly of wet meadows, moors and bogs, on the wing in a single flight during June and July, at low elevations in the north but up to 2,000 metres in the mountains of southern Europe. Much less common in Britain now than in the past, probably as a result of improved land drainage. Found in isolated colonies in most of Europe, including Britain but excluding Arctic Scandinavia and south-western and south-eastern Europe. Occurs also in northern Asia and North America.
The caterpillar is green, spotted with white, and striped with dark green and white. It feeds on Beak-sedge (*Rhynchospora*) and other Grass-family plants, and overwinters at the base of the foodplant.
The chrysalis is green, spotted with white, and is attached to the foodplant.
Identification Resembles the Small Heath (*C.pamphilus*), but on the upper side has a wider grey band along the outer edge of the wings.

Eye-spots are typical not only of this Large Heath butterfly but of Browns (Satyridae) in general. They may be a means of protection and frighten away insectivorous birds and other enemies.

SMALL HEATH
Coenonympha pamphilus
27-34 mm. On the wing, usually in two or more generations, from April onwards, often settling on flowers or on the ground. A common species of grassy places from sea-level to 2,000 metres in western Asia and most of Europe, including Britain but not the extreme north of Scandinavia.
The caterpillar is green, spotted with white, and striped with darker green, and feeds on various species of Grass. In northern Europe some caterpillars from each generation overwinter.
The chrysalis is green and brown, and is attached to the foodplant.
Identification Smaller than the Large Heath (*C.tullia*), and on the upper side has a narrower grey band at the edges of the wings.

CORSICAN HEATH
Coenonympha corinna
25-28 mm. Confined to the Mediterranean islands of Corsica and Sardinia, where it flies from May onwards
in a series of generations. Most common at about 1,000 metres on grassy
mountain slopes.
The caterpillar is green, striped with
dark green and yellow, and feeds on
Sedges (*Carex*) and other Grass-family
plants. It probably overwinters.   .
The chrysalis is reddish-grey, marked
with white.
Identification A distinctively marked
species, especially on the upper side
of the forewing.

DUSKY HEATH
Coenonympha dorus
32-34 mm. Locally common in dry,
rocky places up to about 2,000 metres
in Spain, Italy and southern France,
but found only between 1,500 and
1,800 metres in North Africa. The
single yearly flight usually emerges
in June or July.
The caterpillar feeds on Fescues
(*Festuca*), Bents (*Agrostis*) and other
Grasses. It overwinters.
The chrysalis is not known.
Identification A variable butterfly, but
the colour-pattern of the wings is
generally distinctive.

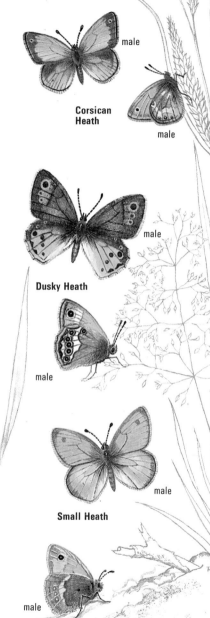

male

Corsican Heath

male

male

Dusky Heath

male

Large Heath

male

male

Small Heath

male

male

83

PEARLY HEATH
Coenonympha arcania
35-40 mm. A generally common butterfly of meadows, in or near woodlands, between 1,000 and 1,200
metres. On the wing during June,
July and August in a single flight.
Found from sea-level to 2,000 metres
in much of Europe, but not Britain,
the Low Countries or Norway. Occurs
also in temperate Asia as far east as
the Ural mountains.
The caterpillar is green, striped along
the body with dark green, white and
yellow. It overwinters, partly grown,
on the foodplant, Melic (*Melica*) and
other Grasses.
The chrysalis is green or brownish-
red, marked with brown.
Identification Similar to the Alpine
Heath (*C.gardetta*), but the eye-spots
are clearly edged with yellow on the
underside of the hind wing.

ALPINE HEATH
Coenonympha gardetta
29-32 mm. Occurs in high meadows
in the Alps and northern Balkans,
seldom lower than 1,500 metres.
Often common in a single flight between June and August.
The caterpillar and **chrysalis** are not
known.
Identification Separable from the
similar Pearly Heath (*C.arcania*) by
the lack of yellow around the eye-
spots under the hind wing.

CHESTNUT HEATH
Coenonympha glycerion
32-35 mm. Common in places, but
usually restricted to wet meadows in
or near woods. Appears in a single
flight during June and July, at low
elevations in the north but up to 2,000
metres in the Alps. Found in Europe
(except Britain, Scandinavia and the
Low Countries), and across Asia to
Siberia.
The caterpillar is green, striped with
dark green and white, and feeds on
False Brome (*Brachypodium*) and
other Grasses. It overwinters.
The chrysalis is green, spotted with
white.
Identification Varies considerably in
colour-pattern, but generally separable from the Alpine Heath (*C.gard-*

Alpine
Heath

etta) by the narrower white band
under the hind wing.

SCARCE HEATH
Coenonympha hero
31-35 mm. Found in widely separated
colonies in meadows and on moors,
and sometimes common in June and
July, when the yearly flight emerges.
Males usually appear several days
before the females. Resident in
northern Europe, but not in Britain,
and across northern Asia to Japan.
The caterpillar is green. It feeds and
overwinters on Lyme Grass (*Elymus
arenarius*) and other Grasses.
The chrysalis is not known.
Identification A variable species.
Some specimens resemble the False
Ringlet (*C.oedippus*), but most are
distinguished by the colour-pattern
of the upper side of the wings.

FALSE RINGLET
Coenonympha oedippus
32-34 mm. Becoming more rare as its
natural habitats, bogs and marshy
meadows, are drained. Emerges in a
single flight during June and July.
Found in widely separated colonies
at low elevations in western France
and across central Europe and temperate Asia to Japan.
The caterpillar, which overwinters, is
green, striped with yellow, and feeds
on Sedges (*Carex*), other Grass-family
plants and on Yellow Flag (*Iris pseud-
acorus*).
The chrysalis is olive-green, marked
with yellow, white and brown.
Identification A generally distinctively
marked butterfly, although some
specimens of the Scarce Heath
(*C.hero*) are fairly similar in overall
appearance.

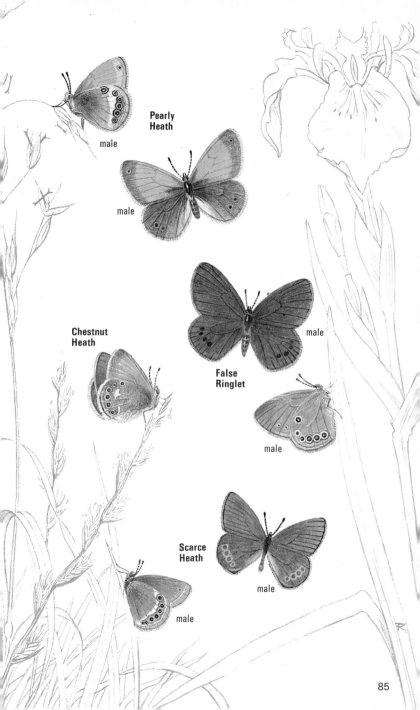

Pearly Heath

male

male

Chestnut Heath

False Ringlet

male

male

Scarce Heath

male

male

SPECKLED WOOD
Pararge aegeria
35-45 mm. A butterfly of woodlands and old hedgerows, where its colour-pattern makes it difficult to see in broken sunlight. Flies in a series of generations from March onwards, but with only one flight in parts of Scandinavia. Found in North Africa, Madeira, the Canaries, most of Europe (except for northern Scotland and northern Scandinavia), and across Asia to the Ural mountains.

The caterpillar is green, striped with dark green and yellow, and feeds on Couch Grass (*Agropyron*) and other Grasses. Some of the Autumn generation overwinter as caterpillars, others in the chrysalis stage.

The chrysalis is green or brown, marked with black and brown, and is attached to the foodplant.

Identification A distinctively patterned species not likely to be confused with any other European butterfly.

WALL BROWN
Lasiommata megera
35-40 mm. Prefers sunny, dry places and often basks in the sunshine on a wall, rock or pathway. Attracted to *Buddleia* and other garden flowers. Often common up to about 1,200 metres from March onwards, usually in two or more generations. Found in Europe (including Britain, but excluding northern Scandinavia), North Africa, Madeira, the Canaries and western Asia.

The caterpillar is blue-green, striped along the body with dark green and white, and feeds on Cocksfoot (*Dactylis glomerata*) and other Grasses. Autumn caterpillars overwinter, some feeding throughout the winter.

The chrysalis is usually green, spotted with white, and is attached to the foodplant.

Identification Separable from the Large Wall Brown (*L.maera*) chiefly by the presence of two dark-brown bars across the cell on the upper side of the forewing.

LARGE WALL BROWN
Lasiommata maera
44-54 mm. Common in rocky, grassy places in or near woodlands, up to about 2,000 metres in the Alps. The single northern and high-elevation flight is in June and July, but there are two generations on the wing elsewhere between May and September. Resident in North Africa, much of Europe (but not Britain), and in western Asia as far east as the Himalayas.

The caterpillar is green, striped with white and dark green, and feeds on various species of Grasses. Autumn generation caterpillars overwinter.

The chrysalis is black or green, dotted with yellow. It is attached to the foodplant or neighbouring plants.

Identification Separable from the smaller Wall Brown (*L.megera*) by the presence of only one dark bar across the cell on the forewing. The Northern Wall Brown (*Lasiommata petropolitana*, not illustrated), is very similar to the Large Wall Brown in colour-pattern but is generally smaller.

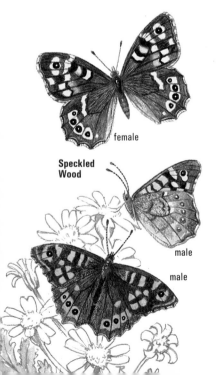

female

Speckled Wood

male

male

WOODLAND BROWN
Lopinga achine

48-54 mm. Occurs in widely separated
colonies up to 1,000 metres in woodland meadows and along edges of
woods in central and northern Europe
(excluding Britain and north-western
Germany), and across temperate Asia
to Japan. Appears in a single flight
between June and August, the males
emerging before the females.

The caterpillar is green, striped with
dark green and white, and feeds on
Rye-grass (*Lolium*), various other
Grasses and Sedges (*Carex*). It overwinters.

The chrysalis is green, striped and
spotted with white.

Identification The large yellow-ringed
spots on the wings separate this
species from all other ·European
Browns.

Woodland
Brown

female

male

Wall Brown

male

Large
Wall
Brown

male

Large
Wall
Brown

male

METALMARKS AND OTHERS
Family Riodinidae

Mainly a Central and South American group but also represented in North America, tropical Africa and Asia, and by a single Fritillary-like species in Europe. Most are small or medium in size. The front leg is much reduced, as in the Nymphalidae, but the family is probably more closely related to the Lycaenidae. Many species are very colourful or have shiny metallic markings on the wings. Males differ little in colour-pattern from the females; upper and underside patterns are usually different. The caterpillars are slug-like in shape and rather hairy.

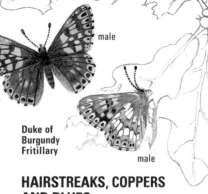

Duke of Burgundy Fritillary

male

male

DUKE OF BURGUNDY FRITILLARY
Hamearis lucina
27-34 mm. Flies in woodland clear-ings and along the edges of woods, during May and June in a single northern generation, or from May to August in the south where there are two flights. Usually rests on a leaf, but is sometimes attracted to Bugle (*Ajuga reptans*) flowers. Found in Spain, Sweden, much of central Europe (not the Low Countries), and in western Asia. Prefers limestone regions in Britain and is absent from Ireland and northern Scotland.
The caterpillar is brown, marked with brown and black, and feeds on Prim-rose (*Primula vulgaris*) and other species of *Primula*.
The chrysalis is brown, spotted with black. It overwinters.
Identification Differs from other Euro-pean Fritillaries in the colour-pattern of the underside of the hind wing.

HAIRSTREAKS, COPPERS AND BLUES
Family Lycaenidae

A worldwide group of several thousand, mainly small species, best represented in the tropics of the Old World but with about 100 species in Europe. The wings are mostly blue, green, brown, orange or red above, but usually very differently coloured on the underside. Most Hairstreaks have one or more short tails to the hind wing. All three pairs of legs are fully developed. Females usually differ from the males in colour-pattern.

The caterpillars are slug-like in shape, and many have a honeygland on the back. Ants are attracted by the sugary secretion of this gland, and probably ward off other insects that might attack the caterpillar. Some caterpillars are taken by the ants into their nest, where the captives feed on the ants' grubs. Other caterpillars feed on aphids, leaf-hoppers and scale-insects. The chrysalis is short and stout, and either hangs from its tail end, supported by a girdle of silk, or lies flat on the ground.

male

Brown Hairstreak

female

BROWN HAIRSTREAK
Thecla betulae

34-36 mm. This butterfly normally flies high up amongst the branches of Oak trees, but is sometimes attracted to flowers at ground level. Appears in August and September in a single flight, and is fairly common locally up to 1,500 metres in central and northern Europe (including Ireland and southern England), and across northern Asia to the Pacific. Overwinters in the egg stage.

The caterpillar is green, striped with yellow, and feeds chiefly on Blackthorn (*Prunus spinosa*).

The chrysalis is brown, and is formed under the leaf of a foodplant.

Identification The under-surface pattern of this species is distinctive.

The lined underside and tailed hind wing of the Brown Hairstreak are common to many Hairstreaks. The upper-surface pattern is strikingly different.

female

Purple Hairstreak

male

male

male

Spanish Purple Hairstreak

male

PURPLE HAIRSTREAK
Quercusia quercus
24-29 mm. Emerges in a single flight between June and August, and often common in Oak forests, flying high up in the trees but occasionally attracted to flowers near the ground. Found in North Africa, western Asia and much of Europe, including Britain but excluding Arctic Scandinavia. Overwinters in the egg stage.
The caterpillar is brown, marked with black and white, and looks rather like the Oak buds (*Quercus*) on which it feeds.
The chrysalis is reddish-brown, spotted with violet-brown, and is formed inside a frail cocoon, either in a crevice of the bark or on the ground.
Identification Separable in both sexes from the Spanish Purple Hairstreak by the markings on the underside, and in the male by the more purplish colour of the upper surface.

SPANISH PURPLE HAIRSTREAK
Laeosopis roboris
30-34 mm. Can be very common in Spain in open woodlands and scrubland, flying between May and August, probably in a single generation. Often attracted to Privet flowers. Found only in Spain, Portugal and southern France, and seldom above 1,500 metres. Overwinters in the egg stage.
The caterpillar is brown, marked with black and yellow, and feeds on various species of Ash (*Fraxinus*) and on Privet (*Ligustrum vulgare*).
The chrysalis is not known.
Identification More bluish above in the male than the Purple Hairstreak (*Quercusia quercus*), and distinctively marked on the underside of the wings in both sexes.

False Ilex Hairstreak

male

male

Ilex Hairstreak

female

Sloe Hairstreak

FALSE ILEX HAIRSTREAK
Nordmannia esculi
28-31 mm. Appears in a single flight during June, July and August in scrubland and open woodlands, usually where there are Oaks. Found in southern France, Spain, Portugal and North Africa; up to 1,500 metres in Spain and to 1,800 metres in North Africa.
The caterpillar feeds on various species of Oak (*Quercus*) and on species of *Prunus*.
The chrysalis is attached to its foodplant.
Identification Most like the Ilex Hairstreak (*N.ilicis*), but the red spots on the underside of the hind wing are smaller and not edged with black.

ILEX HAIRSTREAK
Nordmannia ilicis
32-37 mm. Locally common on hills with Oak scrub, up to 1,500 metres. Emerges in a single flight during June and July. Found in southern and central Europe eastwards to the Balkans, Turkey and the Middle East.
The caterpillar, which overwinters under a leaf, is green, striped with dark green and yellow. It feeds on Oaks (*Quercus*) and other trees, and is often attended by ants.
The chrysalis is brown or grey, and formed close to the ground at the base of the tree.
Identification Differs from the Sloe Hairstreak (*N.acaciae*) in the larger size and by the black-edged red spots on the underside of the wings.

SLOE HAIRSTREAK
Nordmannia acaciae
28-33 mm. Usually found near Blackthorn bushes (*Prunus spinosa*) in dry sunny places during June and July in a single flight. Generally uncommon, and prefers hilly country up to 1,500 metres. Resident in southern Europe and western Asia.
The caterpillar is green, striped with yellow, and feeds on Blackthorn and various species of Oak (*Quercus*). It overwinters.
The chrysalis is attached to the foodplant.
Identification Resembles the Ilex Hairstreak (*N.ilicis*), but differs on the underside of the hind wing.

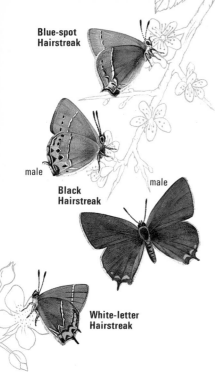

Blue-spot Hairstreak

male

Black Hairstreak

male

White-letter Hairstreak

BLUE-SPOT HAIRSTREAK
Strymonidia spini
27-32 mm. Most often seen in hilly country up to 1,800 metres where there are patches of Buckthorn and Blackthorn. Appears in a single flight between June and early August in central and southern Europe (but not southern Italy), and across temperate Asia to Korea. Overwinters in the egg stage.
The caterpillar is green, striped with yellow and white. It feeds mainly on Blackthorn (*Prunus spinosa*), Buckthorn (*Rhamnus catharticus*), and Hawthorns (*Crataegus*), but also on other shrubs, and is usually attended by ants.
The chrysalis is brown, and is attached to a twig of the foodplant.
Identification The blue mark on the underside at the rear angle of the hind wing separates this species from all other European Hairstreaks. Females are much like the males in colour-pattern.

BLACK HAIRSTREAK
Strymonidia pruni
29-33 mm. Usually found near the edges of Oak woods or along old, overgrown hedgerows, often visiting Bramble (*Rubus*) flowers. The single flight is in May, June and July. Commonest at low elevations, but found up to 1,000 metres in northern and central Europe (including England and southern Scandinavia), and across northern Asia to the Pacific coast. Overwinters in the egg stage.
The caterpillar is at first yellow and brown, rather bud-like in appearance, but later mostly green. It feeds on the buds and leaves of Blackthorn (*Prunus spinosa*) and other species of *Prunus*. It is not attended by ants.
The chrysalis is brown and white, and is secured to a twig of the foodplant.
Identification Both sexes are similar to the White-letter Hairstreak (*S. w-album*) but lack a W-shaped marking under the hind wing and have a row of orange spots on the upper side of the hind wing.

WHITE-LETTER HAIRSTREAK
Strymonidia w-album
24-38 mm. Sometimes common where there are Elm and Lime trees, flying amongst the branches during June, July and August in a single yearly emergence. Found in Europe (not Ireland, Scotland or Portugal), seldom above 1,000 metres, and across temperate Asia to Japan. Overwinters in the egg stage.
The caterpillar is greenish-yellow and green, and feeds on the buds, flowers and leaves of Elms (*Ulmus*) and Limes (*Tilia*).
The chrysalis is brown, and is attached to a leaf or twig of the foodplant.
Identification Separable from the Black Hairstreak (*S.pruni*) by the distinct white W-shaped line under the hind wing, and by the lack of orange on the upper side of the hind wing. The female is similar to the male but a slightly lighter brown above.

GREEN HAIRSTREAK
Callophrys rubi
25-30 mm. A well-camouflaged butterfly when the wings are closed and the green of the underside blends with a background of green leaves. Appears between April and July in a single flight, and is generally common along overgrown hedgerows, thickets and the edges of woods from sea-level up to about 2,000 metres. Widely distributed in Europe (including Britain and the Arctic), North Africa, temperate Asia and North America.

The caterpillar is green and yellow, and feeds on the buds and shoots of gorse (*Ulex*), *Vaccinium* and other shrubs and low-growing plants.

The chrysalis is brown and black, and is formed on the ground or in a bark crevice. It overwinters.

Identification Resembles Chapman's Green Hairstreak (*C.avis*), but the front of the head is green, and the white line on the underside of the hind wing is less complete.

CHAPMAN'S GREEN HAIRSTREAK
Callophrys avis
26-30 mm. A rare butterfly usually found where there are Strawberry Trees, and restricted to North Africa, Portugal, Spain and southern France up to 1,500 metres. There is a single emergence during April and May.

The caterpillar, which is usually attended by ants, feeds on the leaves of Strawberry Tree (*Arbutus unedo*) and, less commonly, on other shrubs.

The chrysalis is formed at the base of the foodplant. It overwinters.

Identification Separable from the Green Hairstreak by the yellow or brownish-red front to the head and by the more complete white line under the hind wing. There is no obvious colour-pattern difference between the sexes.

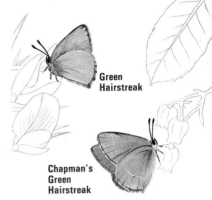

Green Hairstreak

Chapman's Green Hairstreak

PROVENCE HAIRSTREAK
Tomares ballus
22-28 mm. Confined to North Africa, Spain, Portugal and southern France, and found in small colonies in uncultivated, stony countryside and old vineyards, usually at low elevations but in places as high as 1,500 metres. Emerges in a single flight from January onwards in the lowlands, but not until April at higher elevations.

The caterpillar is marked with white, red, blue and purple. It feeds on Birdsfoot Trefoils (*Lotus*), and is attended by ants.

The chrysalis, which overwinters, is reddish-brown in colour.

Identification Unlike any other European butterfly in colour-pattern.

female

Provence Hairstreak

male

male

The beautiful Small Copper is typical of its group. Coppers are allied to both the Blues and Hairstreaks but resemble Blues in underside pattern.

SMALL COPPER
Lycaena phlaeas
25-30 mm. A common butterfly of dry fields and heaths, often visiting flowers or chasing away other butterflies in quick darting flights. The first European emergence is in April or May, the second in July and August, and there is sometimes a third flight, except in the north. Found in most of Europe, up to 2,000 metres, and in North and central Africa, the Canaries, Madeira, temperate Asia (including Japan), and North America.

The caterpillar is green, spotted with white and usually also with red. It feeds on Sorrel (*Rumex*) and Knotgrass (*Polygonum*), and overwinters either partly or full-grown.

The chrysalis is yellow-brown, marked with brown and black.

Identification Separable from other Coppers by colour-pattern details of both surfaces of the wings. The forewing of the female is more rounded than that of the male.

male

Small Copper

male

VIOLET COPPER
Lycaena helle
25-31 mm. Becoming less common as its habitats (bogs and marshes) are drained. On the wing in one or two flights between May and October. Occurs in central and northern Europe (excluding Britain but including the Arctic), up to 1,600 metres in the south but at low elevations in the north. Found also in temperate Asia eastwards to the Pacific.

The caterpillar is green, striped with dark green and yellow, and feeds on Knotgrass (*Polygonum*) and on Sorrels and Docks (*Rumex*).

The chrysalis is yellowish-brown, marked with black. It overwinters.

Identification The male has a distinctive, violet upper side; the strongly marked female is equally distinct from other western European Coppers.

LARGE COPPER
Lycaena dispar
34-40 mm. Small colonies of this colourful species still flourish at low elevations in marshy land in central Europe and temperate Asia, but improved land drainage has greatly depleted its numbers. Native British Large Coppers became extinct during the last century, but Dutch specimens were successfully introduced into eastern England. The single yearly emergence is in June and July.

The caterpillar is green, striped with darker green, and feeds on Docks (*Rumex*), often attended by ants. It overwinters in a rolled leaf, and can withstand being submerged under water without ill effects.

The chrysalis is yellow and brown, striped with brown, and spotted with black and white, and is attached to the foodplant.

Identification Similar to the Scarce Copper (*Heodes virgaureae*, page 96), but has a different underside colour-pattern.

female

Violet Copper

male

male

male

male

Large Copper

female

male

95

female

male

Purple-edged Copper

male

male

Scarce Copper

male

female

PURPLE-EDGED COPPER
Palaeochrysophanus hippothoe
32-34 mm. Generally rare and local in marshy meadows and bogs, up to 2,000 metres in the south, but only at low elevations in Scandinavia. Appears between May and July in a single flight, often resting on Knotgrass (*Polygonum*). Found in most parts of Europe, but absent from Britain, and is becoming rarer elsewhere in Europe. Occurs also across Asia to Siberia and eastern China.
The caterpillar is green, striped with light grey and dark green, and feeds on Docks (*Rumex*) and Knotgrass. It overwinters partly grown.
The chrysalis is yellow, spotted with black, and is formed at the base of a foodplant.
Identification Males are distinctively marked above, with a violet sheen to the hind wing. Females resemble female Purple-shot Coppers (*Heodes alciphron*), but have the row of black spots just beyond the cell arranged in a regular line.

SCARCE COPPER
Heodes virgaureae
32-35 mm. Locally distributed at low elevations in the north and up to 2,000 metres in the Alps in woodland meadows and more open, grassy places, especially near water. On the wing during June, July and August in a single flight. Probably bred in Britain over 200 years ago but now extinct. Absent also in western France and Holland, but found in much of central and northern Europe, including the Arctic, and across temperate Asia to Mongolia. Overwinters in the egg stage.
The caterpillar is green, striped with yellow, and feeds on Sheep's Sorrel (*Rumex acetosella*) and other species of *Rumex*. It is often attended by ants.
The chrysalis is brown, marked with darker brown.
Identification Similar above to the Large Copper (*Lycaena dispar*, page 95), but has white markings on the underside of the hind wing.

SOOTY COPPER
Heodes tityrus
28-33 mm. At high elevations there is
a single flight between June and September, but below 1,000 metres there
are two flights, the first during April
and May and a second in August and
September. Found in meadows, woodland clearings and grassy hillslopes
in central and southern Europe (not
Britain or most of Scandinavia), and
across temperate Asia to western
Mongolia.
The caterpillar is green or violet,
spotted with white. It feeds on Greenweeds (*Genista*), Docks (*Rumex*) and
other plants, and is usually attended
by ants. Autumn caterpillars overwinter.
The chrysalis is either green or brown,
spotted with darker green or brown.
Identification Both sexes are distinctively marked and easily separated
from other European Coppers.

PURPLE-SHOT COPPER
Heodes alciphron
30-36 mm. Found in both damp and
dry, grassy places, often in hilly country. Locally common up to 1,800
metres in the Alps, and higher in the
Atlas mountains of North Africa. On
the wing, probably in a single flight,
between May and August, often visiting Thyme (*Thymus*) and Bramble
(*Rubus*) flowers. Found in North
Africa, central and southern Europe
(not Britain or Scandinavia), and
across temperate Asia to Mongolia.
The caterpillar is green, striped with
light green. It feeds on Sorrels and
Docks (*Rumex*), often with ants in at-
tendance, and hibernates from about
September onwards.
The chrysalis is brownish-green, spotted and striped with darker green,
and is formed near the ground inside
a flimsy cocoon.
Identification Males are fairly distinctive. Females resemble female Purple-
edged Coppers (*Palaeochrysophanus
hippothoe*), but the row of black spots
at the end of the cell on the forewing
is irregular in arrangement.

male

male

**Sooty
Copper**

female

male

Purple-shot Copper

female

male

LONG-TAILED BLUE
Lampides boeticus
24-36 mm. Regularly migrates to northern Europe, including Britain, and has been caught above 3,000 metres on Mount Everest, but never overwinters successfully north of the Alps or in cold climates probably because there is no hibernating phase in the life-history. Flies in Europe in open grassy country and fields of Lucerne (*Medicago sativa*) from June to October as two generations, but has successive flights in warmer regions, where it is a pest of Beans (*Vicia*) and Peas (*Pisum*). Found in southern Europe, temperate Asia (including Japan), Africa, Australia, and in Hawaii.

The caterpillar is green, striped with yellow and dark green, and feeds on the flowers and seed pods of Legumes, including Garden Pea (*Pisum*) and Everlasting Pea (*Lathyrus*).

The chrysalis is pale yellow, marked with brown, and is formed inside a silk cocoon spun in a curled dead leaf.

Identification Separable from Lang's Short-tailed Blue (*Syntarucus pirithous*) by the white band near the margin on the underside of the hind wing. The female is mostly brown above, but violet-blue towards the base of the wings.

LANG'S SHORT-TAILED BLUE
Syntarucus pirithous
23-26 mm. Found on heaths, grassy slopes up to 3,000 metres and in gardens, in several generations from March onwards. Restricted as a year-long resident to North Africa, southern Europe, Turkey and the Middle East, but migrates northwards during the summer.

The caterpillar, which overwinters, is greyish-red, striped with dark brown, and feeds on Broom (*Cytisus*), Gorse (*Ulex*) and other Legumes.

The chrysalis is yellowish-brown.

Identification Similar to the Long-tailed Blue (*Lampides boeticus*), but differs in the absence of a white band under the hind wing.

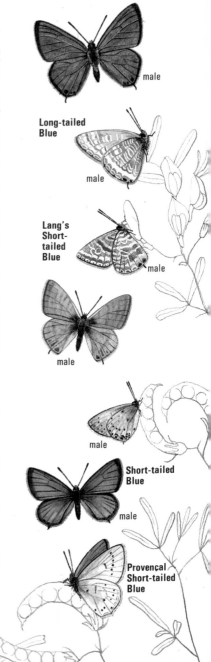

Long-tailed Blue
male

male

Lang's Short-tailed Blue
male

male

male

Short-tailed Blue
male

Provençal Short-tailed Blue

SHORT-TAILED BLUE
Everes argiades

20-32 mm. On the wing in two or three flights from April to September in meadows, pastures and open, un-cultivated country up to about 2,000 metres. Resident in central and south-eastern Europe, across Asia to Japan, and in North America. Migrates north-wards during the summer, and some-times reaches northern continental Europe and Britain.

The caterpillar is at first green but becomes brown during hibernation. It feeds on the flowers and seeds of Gorse (*Ulex*), Medick (*Medicago*) and other Legumes.

The chrysalis is green and black, and is formed in a curled dead leaf of the foodplant.

Identification Both sexes are similar to the Provençal Short-tailed Blue (*E. alcetas*), but on the underside have orange crescent-shaped markings along the margin of the hind wing. Females are mainly dark brown above, but with some blue at the base of the wings.

Escher's Blue (see page 111) is typical of many Blues in its colour-pattern. Generally, males are mostly blue above, and females brown, but both sexes have a similar underside colour-pattern. The male illustrated here is drinking from a wet patch and may be obtaining chemicals that it needs in this way.

PROVENÇAL SHORT-TAILED BLUE
Everes alcetas

28-30 mm. A common butterfly in dry, flowery places up to 1,200 metres in Mediterranean Europe and western Asia. Emerges in two or three flights between April and September.

The caterpillar is similar to that of the Short-tailed Blue (*E. argiades*), and feeds on Medick (*Medicago*) and other Legumes. Autumn caterpillars over-winter.

The chrysalis is similar to, but broader than, that of the Short-tailed Blue.

Identification Both sexes are similar to the Short-tailed Blue, but are sep-arated from it by the absence of orange spots under the hind wing.

male

Little Blue

male

Osiris Blue

male

Holly Blue

female

male

Green-underside Blue

Black-eyed Blue

LITTLE BLUE
Cupido minimus
18-28 mm. Usually restricted to chalk and limestone areas up to 2,400 metres, and found in small colonies, separated sometimes by only a 100 metres or so. Flies in June in the north and at high elevations, but has two flights elsewhere between April and August. Occurs in much of Europe, including Britain but excluding the Arctic, and across Asia to the Pacific.

The caterpillar is either green or yellow, striped with pink, and feeds on the flowers and seeds of Kidney Vetch (*Anthyllis vulneraria*) and other Legumes. Autumn caterpillars overwinter amongst the dead flower-heads of the foodplant.

The chrysalis is greyish-yellow, spotted with brown, and is attached to the foodplant or a nearby Grass stem.

Identification Females are similar to the larger Osiris Blue (*C.osiris*), but never have blue on the upper side of the forewing. Males are dark brown, or brown and silvery blue, not violet-blue.

OSIRIS BLUE
Cupido osiris
25-30 mm. A species of the hills and mountains between 500 and 2,000 metres, usually where there is a luxuriant growth of vegetation. Insignificant in appearance and easily overlooked. Flies between April and September in one or two generations, and found in southern Europe, from Spain to the Balkans, and in western and central Asia north of the Himalayas.

The caterpillar feeds on Mountain Sainfoin (*Onobrychis montana*) and other species of *Onobrychis*. Autumn caterpillars overwinter.

The chrysalis is not known.

Identification Males differ from the Little Blue (*C.minimus*) in the violet upper side; females are difficult to separate from the Little Blue, but sometimes have violet scales on the otherwise dark brown upper side of the wings.

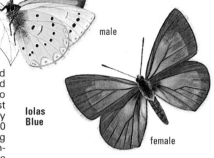
male

Iolas
Blue

female

HOLLY BLUE
Celastrina argiolus
20-32 mm. Widely distributed and common in gardens, heaths and along hedgerows; usually in two flights in temperate climates, the first as early as April. Often rests on Ivy and Holly leaves. Found up to 1,500 metres in most of Europe (including Britain), North Africa, North and Central America and much of temperate Asia.
The caterpillar is green, marked with darker and lighter green, and feeds on the shoots, flowers and berries of Holly (*Ilex*), Ivy (*Hedera*), Gorse (*Ulex*), Dogwoods (*Cornus*) and other shrubs.
The chrysalis is brown, marked with darker brown, and is attached to a leaf or twig of the foodplant. Autumn-generation chrysalids overwinter.
Identification Most like the Provençal Short-tailed Blue (*Everes alcetas*, page 99), but lacks tails on the hind wings.

GREEN-UNDERSIDE BLUE
Glaucopsyche alexis
26-34 mm. Rare north of the Alps, but locally common in hilly and mountainous areas up to 1,200 metres, usually in flowery places near woods. Emerges during April, May and June in a single flight in the north and at high elevations, but has two flights elsewhere between April and August. Found in Europe, from the Mediterranean to southern Scandinavia (but absent from Britain except as a rare vagrant), and in North Africa and across temperate Asia to Siberia.
The caterpillar is green or brown, striped with darker brown or green, and feeds on Milk-vetches (*Astragalus*), Broom (*Cytisus*) and other Legumes. Autumn caterpillars overwinter.
The chrysalis is brown.
Identification Resembles the Black-eyed Blue (*G.melanops*) on the upper side of the wings, but European specimens are partly green on the underside of the hind wing. Females are mainly dark brown above, with some blue scales at the base of the wings.

BLACK-EYED BLUE
Glaucopsyche melanops
24-27 mm. A generally rare Mediterranean butterfly found only in North Africa, Spain, Portugal, southern France and Italy on dry heathland and open woodland, up to 1,000 metres in Europe and 2,000 metres in North Africa. Emerges during March, April and May in a single flight.
The caterpillar is green or grey, with darker lines, and feeds on the flowers and seeds of Vetches (*Lotus*), Greenweeds (*Genista*) and other Legumes. It overwinters.
The chrysalis is not known.
Identification Similar to the Green-underside Blue (*G.alexis*), but lacks green under the hind wing.

IOLAS BLUE
Iolana iolas
37-39 mm. Found only locally in widely separated colonies in Europe. Flies in open woodlands and rocky places up to 2,000 metres. The first generation appears during May and June, the second in August and September. Occurs in southern Europe, North Africa and western Asia.
The caterpillar is either green or brown, striped with darker and lighter lines. It feeds on the flowers and seeds of Bladder Senna (*Colutea arborescens*), and is usually attended by ants.
The chrysalis is brown, spotted with black. It overwinters.
Identification A large, distinctively marked butterfly, not likely to be mistaken for other European blues. Females differ from the males in having a broad, brown border on the upper side of the wings.

101

female

Dusky
Large
Blue

male

Alcon
Blue

male

male

Large
Blue

male

Scarce
Large
Blue

male

ALCON BLUE
Maculinea alcon

34-40 mm. On the wing in meadows, marshes and on moors up to 1,800 metres during June and July in a single flight. Locally common in much of Europe but absent from the south of Spain or Italy, Britain and most of Scandinavia.

The caterpillar feeds at first on Gentians (*Gentiana*), but is then collected by ants and taken to their nest. It feeds inside the nest on ant grubs and overwinters there.

The chrysalis is nearly white, and is formed inside the ants' nest.

Identification Similar to the Large Blue (*M.arion*), but on the underside lacks a blue-green area at the base of the hind wing.

LARGE BLUE
Maculinea arion
35-40 mm. Occurs in dry, grassy places up to 2,000 metres, often on south-facing slopes, in much of Europe, but not Britain, where it apparently became extinct in 1979, or in northern Scandinavia. The single yearly flight is in June and July.
The caterpillar feeds at first on Thyme (*Thymus*) flowers, but is later taken by ants into their nest. Here the caterpillar feeds on ant grubs, overwinters in the nest and eventually crawls to freedom as an adult butterfly.
The chrysalis is brownish-white.
Identification Similar to the Alcon Blue (*M.alcon*) and Scarce Large Blue (*M.teleius*), but separated by the blue-green area at the base of the hind wing on the underside. Females resemble the males, but may have larger black markings.

SCARCE LARGE BLUE
Maculinea teleius
32-36 mm. Common in widely separated colonies in marshy lowland areas, but also occurs on wet moors up to 2,000 metres. Appears in a single flight during June, July and August in central Europe from northern Spain and south-western France eastwards across Europe and temperate Asia to Japan.
The caterpillar is brown, spotted with black. It feeds on the flowers of Great Burnet (*Sanguisorba officinalis*) and Bird's-foot Trefoil (*Lotus corniculatus*), but is later taken by ants into their nest, where it overwinters.
The chrysalis is brownish-white.
Identification Separable from European specimens of the Large Blue (*M.arion*) by the lack of blue-green on the underside at the base of the hind wing. Females have a broader, brown border to the upper side of the wings.

DUSKY LARGE BLUE
Maculinea nausithous
33-37 mm. Usually found in marshes along the edges of lakes, often together with the Large Blue (*M.arion*). On the wing during June, July and August in a single flight; commonest at low elevations, but occurs up to 1,200 metres in Spain. Found in central Europe and across Asia to the Ural mountains.
The caterpillar feeds on the flowers of Great Burnet (*Sanguisorba officinalis*), but is later collected by ants and taken into their nest, where it probably feeds on ant grubs. It overwinters inside the nest.
The chrysalis is formed inside the ants' nest.
Identification Resembles the Scarce Large Blue (*M.teleius*), but the underside is brown, and lacks spots along the edge of the wings.

BATON BLUE
Pseudophilotes baton
20-24 mm. Common in dry, grassy places and scrubland on south-facing slopes up to 2,500 metres. Emerges in a single flight at high elevations, but has two flights between April and September in the lowlands. Attracted to wet mud and animal droppings. Found in Europe (except for Britain, Scandinavia and the Low Countries), and across western Asia to northern Pakistan.
The caterpillar is green, marked with purple and white, much like a Thyme (*Thymus*) flower in colour; it feeds on Thyme flowers and leaves, often attended by ants.
The chrysalis is dull yellow and green, and is found on the ground at the base of the foodplant. Autumn-generation chrysalids overwinter.
Identification Males are distinctively pale pastel blue above; females are mainly black.

Baton Blue

male

male

CHEQUERED BLUE
Scolitantides orion
28-32 mm. Found on dry, sunny ground in widely scattered small colonies in southern Europe from Spain to the Balkans (excluding southern Italy), and also in southern Scandinavia and across temperate Asia as far east as Japan. There is one generation on the wing during June and July in the north and the Alps (up to 1,200 metres), but two flights elsewhere between April and August.
The caterpillar is green, marked with purple and black, and feeds on Stonecrops (*Sedum*).
The chrysalis is dull yellow and green, and is formed at the base of the foodplant. Autumn chrysalids overwinter.
Identification Both sexes are separable from other European Blues by the dark upper side and the heavily spotted, white underside.

ZEPHYR BLUE
Plebejus pylaon
27-33 mm. A butterfly of flowery, grassy places from sea-level to 2,000 metres; on the wing probably in a single flight between May and August. Found in central and southern Europe, the Middle East and across temperate Asia to Japan. Overwinters either in the egg or the caterpillar stage.
The caterpillar is green and yellow, striped along the body with yellow and dark green. It feeds on Milkvetches (*Astragalus* and *Oxytropis*).
The chrysalis is yellow-green.
Identification Separable from the Silver-studded Blue (*P. argus*) by the absence of shiny, silvery scales along the margin of the hind wing on the underside.

SILVER-STUDDED BLUE
Plebejus argus
28-34 mm. Sometimes common on sandy heaths and grassland up to 3,000 metres. Emerges as one flight during July or August in the north, but as two flights in the south from May to September. May fly until dusk if the weather is warm. Found in most of Europe, including Britain but excluding Ireland and northern Scandinavia. Overwinters in the egg stage.
The caterpillar is green or brown, striped with purple and white. It feeds on the shoots and flowers of Gorse (*Ulex*), Birdsfoot (*Ornithopus perpusillus*) and other Legumes.
The chrysalis is usually green, and attached to the base of the foodplant.
Identification Separable in the male from the Idas Blue (*Lycaeides idas*) by the wider black borders to the wings, and in the female by the less extensive orange markings on the hind wing.

IDAS BLUE
Lycaeides idas
28-32 mm. Common in small colonies on heaths and pastures up to 2,000 metres during June and July in the north, and in two flights between May and August in the south. Found in Europe from the Mediterranean to the Arctic (but not in Britain), and eastwards to the Altai mountains of central Asia.
The caterpillar is green, striped with brown and white, and feeds on Gorse (*Ulex*) and other Legumes, and on Sea Buckthorn (*Hippophae rhamnoides*). It is attended by ants and later taken to their nest, where it overwinters.
The chrysalis is green, changing later to brown, and is formed inside the ants' nest.
Identification Most like Reverdin's Blue (*L. argyrognomon*), but is generally smaller and has black arrow-shaped inner edges to the orange spots on the underside of the hind wing. Females have a much broader, brown marginal band on the upper side than the males.

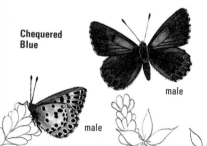

Chequered Blue

male

male

REVERDIN'S BLUE

Lycaeides argyrognomon
24-27 mm. Widespread and common in open, flowery places, especially on mountain slopes up to 1,500 metres. On the wing, usually in two flights, from May to August. Found in central Europe, southern Scandinavia, temperate Asia (including Japan), and in North America. Overwinters in the egg stage.

The caterpillar is green, striped with brown and yellow, and feeds on Crown Vetch (*Coronilla varia*) and probably other Legumes.

The chrysalis is green and yellow.

Identification Both sexes are similar to the Idas Blue (*L.idas*), but the black edges of the orange marginal spots are curved, not pointed, on the underside of the hind wing.

female

Silver-studded Blue

male

male

Zephyr Blue

female

Idas Blue

Reverdin's Blue

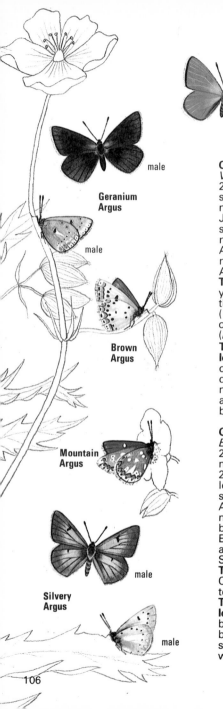

Cranberry Blue

CRANBERRY BLUE
Vacciniina optilete
22-25 mm. Mainly an alpine and Arctic species in Europe, but also found on moors in Germany. Emerges between June and August in a single flight; seldom common, and usually found near the foodplants. Occurs in the Alps and central Germany, across northern Asia to Japan, and in North America.
The caterpillar is green, striped with yellow, white and black, and feeds on the shoots and flowers of Cranberry (*Vaccinium oxycoccus*), other species of *Vaccinium* and on Bell Heathers (*Erica*). It overwinters partly grown.
The chrysalis is green and yellow.
Identification Distinguished from other Arctic and alpine Blues by the deep violet-blue upper side of the male. Females are brown above, with a scattering of violet scales at the base of the wings.

GERANIUM ARGUS
Eumedonia eumedon
23-26 mm. Fairly common in marshy moors and meadows, up to about 2,000 metres in the south, but very local in distribution. On the wing in a single flight during June, July and August. Not present in Britain or north-western continental Europe, but otherwise found in much of Europe, including the Arctic, and across temperate Asia to the eastern Soviet Union.
The caterpillar feeds on species of Cranesbill (*Geranium*), usually attended by ants. It overwinters.
The chrysalis is not known.
Identification Distinctively dark brown (without markings) above in both sexes, and usually with a white stripe on the underside of the hind wing.

BROWN ARGUS
Aricia agestis
24-28 mm. Prefers chalk and limestone areas, and can be locally fairly common on heaths and flowery, grassy slopes up to 1,000 metres in Europe and 1,800 metres in North Africa. There is one flight each year in the north during May and June, but two or more in the south from May to about September. Occurs in the Canary Islands, North Africa, western Asia and much of Europe, including southern England, but not in most of Scandinavia.
The caterpillar is green, striped with dark green, brown, pink and white. It feeds on Storksbill (*Erodium*) and other species of the Geranium family, and is often attended by ants. It overwinters.
The chrysalis is green, striped with pink, and is formed near the base of the foodplant.
Identification The upper-side ground-colour in both sexes is brown. Separable from the female Common Blue (*Polyommatus icarus*, page 113) by the absence of blue scales on the upper side of the wings.

MOUNTAIN ARGUS
Aricia artaxerxes
24-28 mm. A locally common species of grassy slopes and moors, up to 2,000 metres in southern Europe, but at lower elevations in the north. Emerges in a single flight between June and August. Found in North Africa, the mountains of western Europe and the Balkans, in northern Britain and in Scandinavia, including the Arctic.
The caterpillar is like that of the Brown Argus (*A.agestis*), but lacks a white line along the side. It feeds mainly on Rock-rose (*Helianthemum*) and overwinters partly grown.
The chrysalis is slightly paler in colour than that of the Brown Argus.
Identification Similar to the Brown Argus, but has fewer orange spots on the upper side of the forewing.

SILVERY ARGUS
Pseudoaricia nicias
23-25mm. Found between 900 and 2,000 metres in dry, sunny places in the Alps and Pyrenees, and at lower elevations in much of eastern Scandinavia. On the wing during July and August in a single flight. Also present in Asia as far east as the Altai mountains of central Asia. Overwinters in the egg stage.
The caterpillar is green, striped with darker green, and feeds on species of Cranesbill (*Geranium*).
The chrysalis is green, striped with dark green and red. It is attached to the base of the foodplant.
Identification Distinguished by the silvery-blue colour of the male upper side, and by the lack of orange spots on the underside of both sexes. Females are brown above.

ALPINE ARGUS
Albulina orbitulus
23-28mm. A high-meadow butterfly found between 1,500 and 2,800 metres in the central Alps and from 500 to 1,500 metres in Scandinavia. Emerges in a single flight during July and August.
The caterpillar is green, striped with brown and yellowish-green, and feeds on alpine Milk-vetches (*Astragalus*). It overwinters.
The chrysalis is green.
Identification The distinctive underside of this species lacks black markings in both sexes.

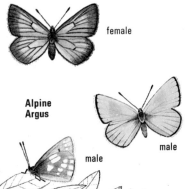

female

Alpine
Argus

male

male

Glandon Blue female

male

Glandon Blue male

Gavarnie Blue male

male

Gavarnie Blue female

GAVARNIE BLUE
Agriades pyrenaicus
21-23 mm. Confined to the Pyrenees, Cantabrian mountains of northern Spain and the mountains of the Balkans between 1,500 and 2,400 metres, and at high elevations in western Asia. A rare species found in small colonies in grassy places, often on limestone soils; on the wing in a single yearly flight during July and August.
The caterpillar which is often attended by ants, feeds on Alpine Snowbell (*Soldanella alpina*) and other species of the Primula family. It overwinters.
The chrysalis is not known.
Identification Resembles the Glandon Blue (*A.glandon*), but has a row of black spots close to the outer margin under the forewing.

GLANDON BLUE
Agriades glandon
25-31mm. A locally common, high mountain species found in grassy places from 1,800 metres up to the snow line in the Alps, Pyrenees and the mountains of southern Spain and the Balkans, but at low elevations in Arctic Scandinavia, Asia, Alaska and Canada. Appears in a single flight during June, July and August.
The caterpillar is green, marked with red and white. At first it bores into the leaves of Alpine Snowbell (*Soldanella alpina*) and other plants, and then eats both flowers and leaves, feeding at night and sheltering under stones during the day and much of the winter.
The chrysalis is grey-brown, marked with yellow, and is hidden under a stone.
Identification Best separated from the similar Gavarnie Blue (*A.pyrenaicus*) by the row of grey spots close to the outer margin on the forewing.

MAZARINE BLUE
Cyaniris semiargus
26-34 mm. A generally common butterfly of open, flowery places, from sea-level to 1,800 metres in Europe, and up to 2,500 metres in the south of its range. Emerges during June and July at high elevations, but has two flights in the lowlands between May and August. Often drinks from wet mud. Resident in North Africa, most of Europe (but not Britain, except as a rare migrant) and across temperate Asia to the Pacific.
The caterpillar is yellow-green, striped with green, and feeds on Trefoils (*Lotus*) and other Legumes. Autumn caterpillars overwinter.
The chrysalis is yellow, spotted with brown, and is formed inside a frail cocoon attached to the foodplant.
Identification Rather similar to the Osiris Blue (*Cupido osiris*, page 100), but the underside is darker and more brownish in colour. The female is brown above.

TURQUOISE BLUE
Plebicula dorylas
28-31 mm. A butterfly of grassy places with some trees or shrubs, commonest between 1,000 and 2,000 metres, but very locally distributed. On the wing from May to September in two flights, except at high elevations, where there is a single flight in midsummer. Found in much of Europe, except for Britain, north-western continental Europe and the Arctic. Occurs also in Turkey.

The caterpillar is green, marked with darker green and yellow, and feeds on the buds and flowers of Thyme (*Thymus*) and on various species of Legumes, often attended by ants. It overwinters on the foodplant.

The chrysalis is not known.

Identification Very similar to the Mother-of-pearl Blue (*P.nivescens*), but males are a more intense blue above, and most females lack orange spots on the forewing.

MOTHER-OF-PEARL BLUE
Plebicula nivescens
26-28 mm. Although found in France in the eastern part of the Pyrenees, this is mainly a Spanish butterfly. Occurs on grassy slopes and in meadows near woods or scrubland between 1,000 and 1,800 metres. Appears in a single flight during June and July.

The caterpillar, which overwinters, feeds on Clovers (*Trifolium*) and other Legumes.

The chrysalis is not known.

Identification Resembles the Turquoise Blue (*P.dorylas*), but the male is silvery blue above, and the female usually has orange spots on the upper side of the forewing.

Turquoise Blue
male

male

female

Mother-of-pearl Blue
male

male

female

Mazarine Blue

DAMON BLUE
Agrodiaetus damon
30-35 mm. A rare mountain butterfly found in small colonies up to 3,000 metres in grassy places or light scrub on chalk or limestone soils. Flies during June, July and early August in a single generation. Occurs in the Pyrenees, Alps, Apennines and the mountains of the Balkans and western Asia as far east as western Mongolia.
The caterpillar, which overwinters, is yellowish-green, striped with dark green, yellow and red. It feeds on the flowers of Sainfoin (*Onobrychis*), and is attended by ants.
The chrysalis is dull yellow.
Identification Both sexes resemble the Furry Blue (*A.dolus*), but lack a white streak on the underside of the hind wing. The female is brown above.

FURRY BLUE
Agrodiaetus dolus
30-34 mm. Common in small colonies at low elevations and up to 1,800 metres in uncultivated, open country. Emerges in July and August in a single flight. Known only from northern Spain, southern France and Italy.
The caterpillar is green, striped with yellow and dark green. It feeds mainly on Sainfoin (*Onobrychis*), often attended by ants, and overwinters.
The chrysalis is not known.
Identification Males have a distinctive, furry brown patch on the forewing; females are completely brown above. Both sexes have a conspicuous white stripe on the underside of the hind wing.

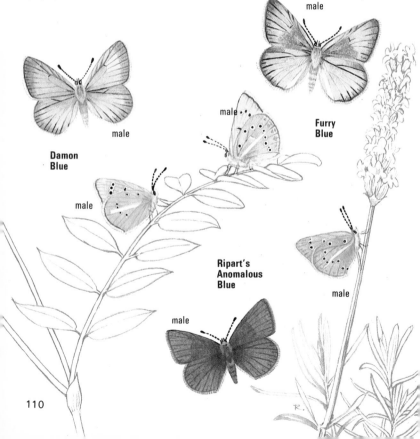

male

Furry Blue

male

Damon Blue

male

male

Ripart's Anomalous Blue

male

male

110

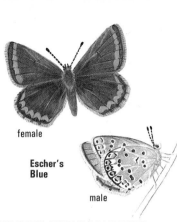

female

Escher's
Blue

male

Amanda's
Blue

male

Amanda's Blue

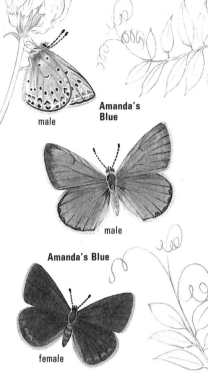

female

RIPART'S ANOMALOUS BLUE
Agrodiaetus ripartii
26-31 mm. On the wing in a single flight during June, July and August in stony places, often settling on the flowers of Lavender (*Lavandula*). Locally common from the lowlands to 1,600 metres. Found in Spain, southern France, Italy, the Balkans and Turkey.

The caterpillar, which overwinters, feeds on Sainfoin (*Onobrychis*).

The chrysalis is not known.

Identification Both sexes are dark brown above, distinctively streaked with greyish-white beneath, and are easily separated from all other western European Blues.

ESCHER'S BLUE
Agrodiaetus escheri
33-35 mm. Locally distributed in dry, rocky places, usually between 300 and 1,500 metres, where it emerges during June, July and August in a single flight. Found in southern Europe, from Spain to the Balkans, and in Turkey and North Africa.

The caterpillar is green, striped with yellow, and feeds on Milk-vetches (*Astralagus*), Thyme (*Thymus*) and other plants, often attended by ants. It overwinters.

The chrysalis is green or yellowish-brown.

Identification Similar to the more widespread Adonis Blue (*Lysandra bellargus*, page 112), but lacks a black spot near the base of the forewing on the underside.

AMANDA'S BLUE
Agrodiaetus amanda
30-35 mm. Fairly common in flowery meadows and hilly scrubland, at low elevations in the north but up to 1,500 metres in the Alps and at higher elevations in North Africa. Flies in one generation during May and June in the north and at high elevations, but has two flights between May and August elsewhere. Occurs in North Africa, western Asia and in much of Europe, but not in Britain, north-western continental Europe or northern Scandinavia.

The caterpillar is green, striped with white and brown, and feeds on Vetches (*Vicia*), usually attended by ants. It overwinters partly grown.

The chrysalis is not known.

Identification Both sexes are large and distinctive.

111

Meleager's Blue

male

male

female

female

Chalk-hill Blue

male

male

MELEAGER'S BLUE
Meleageria daphnis
35-38 mm. Commonest below 1,000 metres on grassy, flowery slopes, but can occur up to 1,800 metres. Found in small colonies in southern Europe, eastwards to Iran, but not in Spain or Portugal.
The caterpillar, which probably over-winters, is green, marked with yellow and black. It feeds on Scorpion Vetches (*Coronilla*), other Legumes and on Thyme (*Thymus*).
The chrysalis is not known.
Identification Unlikely to be confused with any other European species.

CHALK-HILL BLUE
Lysandra coridon
29-36 mm. A common species of chalk and limestone grassland up to 3,000 metres, emerging during July or August. Attracted to flowers and animal droppings. Found in most of Europe but absent from much of the south-west, Ireland, Scotland and Scandinavia.
The caterpillar overwinters on the foodplant as a caterpillar inside the unbroken egg-shell. When full grown it is green, striped with yellow, and feeds at night on the leaves and flowers of Wild Liquorice (*Astragalus glycyphyllos*), and other Legumes, attended by ants.
The chrysalis is yellow-brown and dark brown, and is formed at the base of the foodplant.
Identification Most males differ from the very similar southern European Provence Chalk-hill Blue (*L.hispana*, not illustrated), in the more bluish upper side.

ADONIS BLUE
Lysandra bellargus
30-36 mm. Fairly common in colonies on grassy chalk and limestone regions up to 2,000 metres. The usual two flights are in May and June and August and September. Found in southern England, continental Europe, except for Scandinavia, and eastwards to Iran. Protected by law in France.
The caterpillar is green, striped with yellow, and feeds at night, chiefly on leaves of Horseshoe Vetch (*Hippo-*

crepis comosa). It overwinters, often soon after hatching.

The chrysalis is olive-brown and green, striped with dark brown, and is formed on the ground near the foodplant.

Identification Females may be confused with female Chalk-hill Blues (*L.coridon*), but have blue, not silvery-blue scales on the upper side.

COMMON BLUE
Polyommatus icarus
25-33 mm. The commonest European Blue in grassy, flowery places from the Arctic to the Mediterranean; found also in North Africa, the Canary Islands, and much of temperate Asia. Appears between May and July in the north, but in two or three flights in the south between April and October.

The caterpillar is green, striped with dark green and white, and feeds on Trefoils (*Lotus*) and other Legumes. Autumn-generation caterpillars overwinter at the base of the foodplant in a frail, silken shelter.

The chrysalis is brown and green, and is enclosed in a cocoon attached to the stem of the foodplant near the ground.

Identification Both sexes can be separated from the very similar southern European Chapman's Blue (*Plebicula thersites*, not illustrated), by the presence of a black spot in the cell under the forewing.

EROS BLUE
Polyommatus eros
22-26 mm. A butterfly of grassy places between 1,200 and 2,500 metres; on the wing in a single flight from June to August. Occurs in colonies in the Pyrenees, central France, the Alps, the Apennines, and in eastern Europe and western and central Asia.

The caterpillar, which overwinters, is yellowish-green, striped with dark green and yellow. It feeds on Vetches (*Astragalus* and *Oxytropis*) and other Legumes, often attended by ants.

The chrysalis is not known.

Identification Males are separable from the similar Common Blue (*P.icarus*) by the less violet hue of the upper side; females by the less complete orange spotting.

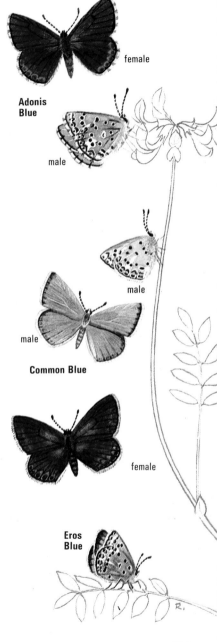

Adonis
Blue

female

male

male

male

Common Blue

female

Eros
Blue

SKIPPERS
Family Hesperiidae

A worldwide family of about 3,000 mostly small species, with about 40 species in Europe. All have a broad head and body, and most make only short, swift, darting flights. The club of the antenna is usually rather pointed and curved; all six legs are well developed. Many are sombrely coloured above, and the underside provides the best guide to identity. Females differ little from the males in colour-pattern. They rest either with the wings folded together above the back or held in a tent-like fashion, as in many moths. The caterpillars have a slight constriction or neck behind the head, and often live in a shelter of silk and leaves. The chrysalis is usually fastened by a silken girdle inside a cocoon.

NORTHERN GRIZZLED SKIPPER
Pyrgus centaureae
22-30 mm. A northern butterfly of bogs, heaths and the sparse vegetation of the Arctic. Emerges in a single flight during June and July, from sea-level up to about 1,000 metres. Found in northern Scandinavia and Asia and in northern North America.
The caterpillar feeds on Cloudberry (*Rubus chamaemorus*).
The chrysalis is not known.
Identification Similar to the Alpine Grizzled Skipper (*P.andromedae*, page 116), but the underside of the hind wing is paler in colour and the veins not so noticeably white.

LARGE GRIZZLED SKIPPER
Pyrgus alveus
28-33 mm. A locally common butterfly in hills and mountains up to about 2,000 metres, especially in grassy valleys. Emerges in a single flight between May and September, but at high elevations usually on the wing in July and August. Found in North Africa, most of Europe (except the Arctic, Britain, north-western Germany and the Low Countries), and across temperate Asia to Siberia.
The caterpillar is brown, striped with dark brown, and feeds on Bramble (*Rubus*), Cinquefoil (*Potentilla*), other plants of the Rose family, and on Rock-rose (*Helianthemum*). Autumn caterpillars overwinter.
The chrysalis is brown, with a blue bloom, and is spotted with black. It is formed inside a frail, silken cocoon.
Identification Very similar to Foulquier's Grizzled Skipper (*P.foulquieri*, not illustrated), and difficult to identify without an examination of internal structures.

male

Northern Grizzled Skipper

male

Large Grizzled Skipper

male   male

OBERTHUR'S GRIZZLED SKIPPER
Pyrgus armoranicus
20-25 mm. Prefers dry, hilly scrubland at low elevations, but occurs up to 1,200 metres in the Alps. Appears in two flights between May and August in most of its range, but may have three flights in the south from May to October. Found in south and central Europe (not Britain), North Africa and western Asia.
The caterpillar is grey, striped with dark grey and red, and feeds on Cinquefoil (*Potentilla*) and Strawberry (*Fragaria*). Autumn caterpillars overwinter.
The chrysalis is not known.
Identification Differs from the Large Grizzled Skipper (*P.alveus*) in the better-marked upper side of the hind wing.

CARLINE SKIPPER
Pyrgus carlinae
20-26 mm. A locally common butterfly from near sea-level to 2,400 metres. Found in southern Europe from Portugal to Austria and Yugoslavia. On the wing from June to September in a single flight.
The caterpillar feeds on Cinquefoil (*Potentilla*), and hibernates from about September to June of the following year.
The chrysalis is not known.
Identification Similar to the Olive Skipper (*P.serratulae*, page 116), but has a characteristic white marking near the outer edge of the hind-wing underside.

ROSY GRIZZLED SKIPPER
Pyrgus onopordi
20-25 mm. Flies in dry, flowery meadows up to 1,500 metres in the Alps and 1,900 metres in the Atlas mountains of North Africa, but commonest at low elevations. There are usually two flights in the north and at high elevations, but three generations elsewhere between April and October. Found in southern Europe from Portugal to Yugoslavia and in North Africa.
The caterpillar feeds on *Malope malacoides*, a species of the Mallow family. Autumn caterpillars overwinter.
The chrysalis is not known.
Identification Much like the Carline Skipper (*P.carlinae*) in colour-pattern, but has a distinctively-shaped white spot at the middle of the rear edge of the hind wing on the underside.

male

Rosy
Grizzled
Skipper

male

female

Carline
Skipper

male

Oberthur's
Grizzled
Skipper

male

male

male

115

OLIVE SKIPPER
Pyrgus serratulae
23-28 mm. On the wing in a single flight during June, July and August in meadows and on grassy slopes near woods. Common and widespread above 1,000 metres and up to 2,400 metres; less common at lower levels. Found in southern and central Europe eastwards through Turkey to the Middle East.

The caterpillar, which overwinters, feeds on Cinquefoils (*Potentilla*) and Lady's Mantle (*Alchemilla*).

The chrysalis is not known.

Identification Very similar in colour-pattern to the Large Grizzled Skipper (*P.alveus*, page 114), but the white markings are more clearly defined on the underside of the hind wing.

YELLOW-BANDED SKIPPER
Pyrgus sidae
26-30 mm. Flies in meadows and open grassland up to 1,500 metres in southern Europe, from southern France and Italy through the Balkans to western Asia. Commonest in the east of its range. Emerges in June and July in a single flight.

The caterpillar probably feeds on species of the Mallow family and has been recorded feeding on the mainly subtropical China Jute (*Abutilon avicennae*).

The chrysalis is not known.

Identification Easily identified by the conspicuously marked white and yellow underside.

GRIZZLED SKIPPER
Pyrgus malvae
20-29 mm. Found in meadows, bogs and forest clearings up to 1,700 metres, and usually fairly common. Often rests at night on grass stems or under flower-heads. There is usually a single flight in the north during May and June, but two flights in the south from April to August. The range includes North America, western Europe (excluding northern Scotland, Ireland and northern Scandinavia), and across temperate Asia to Siberia.

The caterpillar is green, striped with pink and brown, and feeds on Strawberry (*Fragaria*), Mallow (*Malva*) and other plants.

The chrysalis is brown and green, marked with black, and is formed in a silken cocoon attached to the food-plant. It overwinters.

Identification The row of white spots close to the outer margin on the upper side of the forewing separates this species from other European Skippers.

SAFFLOWER SKIPPER
Pyrgus carthami
31-34 mm. Common in places up to 1,500 metres on heaths and grassy scrubland and in meadows. On the wing between June and September, probably in a single generation. Occurs in southern and central Europe, as far north as northern Germany, but not extending to Britain, Ireland or north-western France. Present also in western and central temperate Asia.

The caterpillar feeds on Cinquefoils (*Potentilla*), Safflower (*Carthamus tinctorius*), and Mallow (*Malva*). It overwinters.

The chrysalis is not known.

Identification Very similar to the Large Grizzled Skipper (*P.alveus*, page 114), but on the underside the white spots in the middle of the hind wing are differently placed.

ALPINE GRIZZLED SKIPPER
Pyrgus andromedae
25-28 mm. Rarely found below 1,000 metres and usually seen above 1,500 metres in the Pyrenees, Alps, and Balkan mountains, but at lower levels in Arctic Scandinavia. Inhabits grassy places or heathland, often near streams, and is on the wing in a single flight between May and August.

The caterpillar feeds on Mallow (*Malva*).

The chrysalis is not known.

Identification Resembles the Dusky Grizzled Skipper (*P.cacaliae*), but has larger white spots on the upper side of the forewing.

DUSKY GRIZZLED SKIPPER
Pyrgus cacaliae
21-25 mm. A widespread butterfly of either dry or wet heaths and grassy places in the Pyrenees, Alps and

Balkans; common between 1,600 and 2,500 metres, except in the Pyrenees. There is a single emergence between June and August.

The caterpillar feeds on Coltsfoot (*Tussilago farfara*), Avens (*Geum*) and other plants.

The chrysalis is not known.

Identification See the Alpine Grizzled Skipper (*P.andromedae*).

RED UNDERWING SKIPPER
Spialia sertorius
17-22 mm. Often common in dry, grassy places near woods, especially on chalk and limestone soils, up to about 1,800 metres in the Alps. Appears in two flights; the first during April, May and June, the second between July and September. Found in North Africa, central and southern Europe as far north as Belgium, and across temperate Asia to the eastern Soviet Union.

The caterpillar is brown, striped with black and yellow, and feeds on Burnet (*Sanguisorba*), Cinquefoils (*Potentilla*) and Raspberry (*Rubus*). It overwinters.

The chrysalis is brown, and formed at the base of the foodplant.

Identification Unlikely to be confused with any other western European Skipper.

male

Yellow-banded Skipper

male

Grizzled Skipper

male

male

male

Safflower Skipper

male

male

Alpine Grizzled Skipper

male

Olive Skipper

male

male

Red Underwing Skipper

male

Dusky Grizzled Skipper

male

male

SAGE SKIPPER
Syrichthus proto
24-30 mm. A butterfly of dry open rough country, on the wing in two or three generations throughout the summer from April onwards. Found at low elevations and up to 1,700 metres in North Africa, southern Europe from Portugal to Greece, and in western Asia.
The caterpillar feeds on Horehound (*Marrubium*), species of *Salvia* and other plants. Autumn caterpillars overwinter.
The chrysalis is not known.
Identification A large species with distinctive underside markings.

MALLOW SKIPPER
Carcharodus alceae
22-27 mm. A local, but widely distributed, butterfly of dry, sandy, flowery hillsides up to 1,600 metres in the Alps. There is a single flight during May and June at high elevations, and two or three flights between April and September at lower levels. Found in North Africa, southern and central Europe as far north as Holland, and in western and central temperate Asia.
The caterpillar is grey, striped with black and white, and spotted with yellow or orange. It feeds inside a rolled leaf of Mallow (*Malva*), Tree Mallow (*Lavatera*) or Horehound (*Marrubium*). Autumn caterpillars overwinter.
The chrysalis is brown, with a blue bloom.
Identification Distinctively marked and unlikely to be mistaken for any other Skipper in western Europe.

MARBLED SKIPPER
Carcharodus lavatherae
25-29 mm. Locally distributed on dry slopes, usually in chalk and limestone regions. On the wing usually in a single flight during May, June and July. Found in North Africa, southern Europe (excluding Portugal) and Turkey.
The caterpillar, which overwinters, is grey, striped and speckled with brown and yellow. It feeds on Yellow Woundwort (*Stachys recta*) in a silken web. Autumn caterpillars overwinter.
The chrysalis is brown, with a blue bloom.
Identification Separated from other western European Skippers by the colour-pattern of the upper side.

SOUTHERN MARBLED SKIPPER
Carcharodus boeticus
23-26 mm. Found in isolated colonies on dry, flowery hillsides up to 1,500 metres or above. Occurs in Spain, Portugal, the Alps and through Turkey to Iran. On the wing in two or three generations between May and October.
The caterpillar feeds on species of Horehound (*Marrubium* and *Ballota*). Autumn caterpillars overwinter.
The chrysalis is not known.
Identification Similar to the southern European Tufted Skipper (*C.flocciferus*, not illustrated), but the markings on the underside of the hind wing are in regularly arranged rows.

male

male

male

Mallow Skipper

male

**Sage
Skipper**

male

Marbled Skipper

male

male

Dingy Skipper

male

male

DINGY SKIPPER
Erynnis tages
24-30 mm. Prefers dry, open places and is generally common on heaths and in meadows up to 2,000 metres. Emerges during May and June in the north, or from April to late summer as two generations in the south. Often basks on bare ground, seldom on leaves. Breeds in most of Europe (including Britain, but excluding the Arctic), and in Asia eastwards to Siberia.
The caterpillar is green, and feeds on Trefoils (*Lotus*), Vetches (*Coronilla*) and other Legumes. It overwinters in a silken shelter on the foodplant, changing to a chrysalis in the spring.
The chrysalis is green, brown and yellow.
Identification Separated from other western Europe Skippers by the upper-side colour-pattern and the almost unmarked underside.

male

male

Southern Marbled Skipper

The Large Chequered Skipper is unusually colourful below. Swept-back wings are typical of resting Skippers.

Large Chequered Skipper

LARGE CHEQUERED SKIPPER
Heteropterus morpheus
33-36 mm. Mainly a lowland butterfly, locally distributed in grassy woodland clearings up to about 500 metres. Appears usually in a single flight during June, July and August, but may have two generations in the south. Rare in Scandinavia and absent from mainland Britain, but found in much of Europe and across temperate Asia to the Pacific.
The caterpillar is green or yellow, striped with dark green and white, and feeds on Grasses. Autumn caterpillars overwinter inside a tube of grass and silk.
The chrysalis is green.
Identification Conspicuously marked on the underside and unlikely to be confused with other western European Skippers.

119

CHEQUERED SKIPPER
Carterocephalus palaemon
26-29 mm. Lives in open, lowland grassy places and in woodland mea-

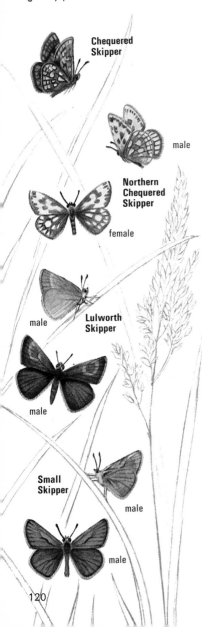

Chequered Skipper

male

Northern Chequered Skipper

female

male Lulworth Skipper

male

Small Skipper

male

male

dows, often near water. Flies from May to July. Extends from the Alps to the Arctic Circle; also in Asia and North America. Rare in Britain.
The caterpillar is yellow-green, and feeds on Brome (*Bromus*) and other Grasses. It overwinters in a silken tube.
The chrysalis is yellow and grey and enclosed in a cocoon of grass and silk.
Identification Separated from the similarly patterned Northern Chequered Skipper (*C.silvicolus*) by the less yellowish ground colour of the wings.

NORTHERN CHEQUERED SKIPPER
Carterocephalus silvicolus
20-25 mm. Commonest in grassy places in damp woods at low elevations. Found in June and July in north-western Europe and temperate Asia.
The caterpillar is brownish-yellow, striped with red. It feeds on Dog's Tail (*Cynosurus*) and other Grasses, and overwinters.
The chrysalis is not known.
Identification Separated from the Chequered Skipper (*C.palaemon*) by the more yellowish colour.

LULWORTH SKIPPER
Thymelicus acteon
22-27 mm. A common grassland species on the wing between June and August up to 1,500 metres in North Africa, Europe as far north as England (but not Scandinavia), and eastwards to Iran.
The caterpillar is green, striped with brown and white, and feeds on Brome (*Bromus*) and other Grasses. It overwinters inside a silk tube.
The chrysalis is green and attached to its foodplant.
Identification Similar to the Small Skipper (*T.flavus*), but usually darker in colour.

SMALL SKIPPER
Thymelicus flavus
25-30 mm. The yearly flight extends from June to September in damp, grassy places up to 1,500 metres. Common locally in North Africa, Britain, southern and central Europe, and east to Iran.

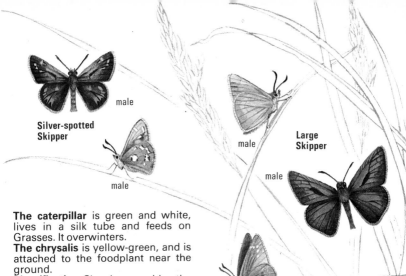

Silver-spotted Skipper
male

male

male

Large Skipper
male

male

Pigmy Skipper

female

The caterpillar is green and white, lives in a silk tube and feeds on Grasses. It overwinters.

The chrysalis is yellow-green, and is attached to the foodplant near the ground.

Identification Closely resembles the Essex Skipper (*T.lineolus*, not illustrated), but the tip of the antenna is orange below, not black.

SILVER-SPOTTED SKIPPER
Hesperia comma
28-31 mm. Locally common in July and August in grassy places, mainly in chalk and limestone areas up to 2,500 metres. Found in North Africa, most of Europe and temperate Asia and in western North America. Overwinters as an egg.

The caterpillar is green and black, lives in a tube of silk and grass, and feeds on Fescues (*Festuca*) and other Grasses.

The chrysalis is enclosed in a cocoon attached to the Grass near the ground.

Identification The silvery spots on the underside separate this species from the other European Skippers.

LARGE SKIPPER
Ochlodes venatus
27-35 mm. Inhabits meadows up to 1,800 metres, flying from May to August in one or more generations. Found in much of Europe, including Britain, and across Asia to Japan.

The caterpillar is mostly green, and lives in a silk tube on Brome (*Bromus*) and other Grasses. It overwinters at the Grass base in a silk shelter.

The chrysalis is grey and black, and is protected by a silk cocoon attached to a Grass stem.

Identification Similar to the Silver-spotted Skipper (*Hesperia comma*), but has yellow spots on the underside.

PIGMY SKIPPER
Gegenes pumilio
26-28 mm. Flies in hot, rocky places, usually at low elevations, between April and October. Locally distributed in small colonies mainly in coastal regions of southern Spain and France, Italy and the Balkans and in North Africa; but is widely distributed in tropical Africa.

The caterpillar feeds on Grasses and possibly on other plants.

The chrysalis is not known.

Identification The wings have few markings unlike those of other western European Skippers.

Index

Butterflies (Scientific Names)

ACKNOWLEDGEMENTS

The author and publishers wish to thank the following for their help in supplying photographs for this book on the pages indicated:

M. Chinery 43, 61; NHPA 21 (Barry Angell), 94 (N.A. Callow), 50 (Stephen Dalton), 99 (M.W.F. Tweedie), 23, 89 (W. Zeph); Natural Science Photos 17 (T. Angermeyer), 119 (Thomas Ruckstuh); R.C. Revels 8, 29, 82.

Picture research by Penny Warn.